When We Pray

By Shirleena Racine

Table of Contents

Foreword

As a minister of the Gospel of Jesus Christ, I often find myself being asked to pray for others. With every request, my response has always been and will be, "Have you prayed first?" Not because I do not want to pray, but because I want to ensure that the requestor believes in the power of prayer. I always pray for and with the requestor, but it is important for everyone to know and understand that God hears them too. Prayer is necessary, just like we need air to breathe and food to eat, along with the many other necessities we need to live. Prayer is our connection to God, a constant connection to the one who sees all and knows all.

To experience this collection of essential prayers is to glimpse into the author, Shirleena Racine, and her awareness of the power of prayer. Through my many years of knowing Shirleena, bonding over the love of God, and wanting to see His people be well in every aspect of life, I have seen and heard her pray these prayers, joined in on a few of them, and watched God answer her requests in ways no one could have ever expected. Prayer works, prayer changes things! Pray regularly, not just out of routine, but because it is a way of life. Prayer creates a covering, like it did for Daniel, where prayer was his custom, praying often, and he was covered by God in the lion's den.

When we pray, we receive clarity; we can not only see clearly in the spiritual, but our physical eyes are opened as well. When we pray, we get accustomed to hearing the voice of God and receiving His directions for us so that we may navigate this thing called life. Shirleena has done an excellent job of cultivating a resource for us as readers to effectively pray even when we cannot find the words.

My prayer for Shirleena is that she keeps doing the work of the Lord. She has answered the God-designed call to be impactful in the lives of others. Keep close in heart 1 Corinthians 15:58 (NKJV), "Therefore, my beloved brethren, be steadfast, immovable, always abounding in the work of the Lord, knowing that your labor is not in vain in the Lord." My prayer for every reader is that you are encouraged through prayer, find peace in prayer, and grow with every prayer.

Be Blessed Always!

-Minister Kandice Williams-Samuel

Dedication

Y'all know that one meme, "But I had a Praying Grandmother" …

I thank God for our ancestors who prayed for us, unsure what the future would hold.
Some knew they would never see our face…
This is book of prayers homage to them.

This book is also a token of gratitude for the active grandmothers that showed us what it looked like to have a life filled with Jesus Christ.
I dedicate this book to my grandmother and favorite person, Ms. Ruby J. Crawford.
I remember how she always had a bible devotional laying around, played "Grace and Mercy" by Mississippi Mass Choir over and over, was up super early for sunrise service, and playing Kirk Franklin's Stomp on repeat.
I loved it all.
Thank you for the hope, the example, and the love you gave me.

Snapping back to reality, "Alexa, play Earth is Ghetto by Aliah Sheffield."
Existing is tiring. There is so much going on and so many unknowns.
But to GOD be the GLORY.
It is our time to learn how to pray and use it as weapon to continue the fight just like our grandmothers did.
I wrote this book as an intentional step to strengthening my relationship with God.
He is needed now, more than ever,
and I pray you use these prayers when you need to.
Seek Him. He is waiting to hear from you.

Matthew 7:7–8 (NIV):

“Ask and it will be given to you; seek and you will find;
knock and the door will be opened to you.
For everyone who asks receives; the one who seeks finds;
and to the one who knocks, the door will be opened.”

How to Use This Book

From Minister Kandice Williams-Samuel:

> "Prayer is a benefit to the relationship we have with God. We have a direct connection through Jesus Christ. The Word of God encourages us to pray. Philippians 4:6-7 reminds us to "Be anxious for nothing, but in everything by prayer and supplication, with thanksgiving, let your requests be made known to God; and the peace of God, which surpasses all understanding, will guard your hearts and minds through Christ Jesus." Prayer provides us with access to communicate without the worry of receiving a busy signal. When we really think about it, even Jesus prayed. The Bible displays several accounts of when Jesus prayed. The disciples even begged Jesus in Matthew to teach them how to pray; we have reference to this teaching through the Lord's Prayer. In our efforts to be more Christ-like, let us pray."

Think of this book as a tool. It is not designed to be read all the way through. Search for a Prayer based off your needs and come back later when you need more.

Each page has a prayer, writing prompt, affirmation, and song. I guarantee life will get better when you develop and grow relationship with God. With daily practice, this can become the start of things to shift, peace found, and identity changed.

There is no wrong way to PRAY. God just wants to hear from you, so make time to share your heart with him. You are encouraged to recite these prayers as they are or make them personal and add identifying words that reflect where you are now in life.

I will say this. Make time for God. EVERY DAY.

This is about YOU building a relationship with Him.

Play, "When I Pray" by DOE

-Shirleena Racine

New Day Means New Mercy

A Prayer for Starting Again

Heavenly Father,
I stand before You ready to begin again, laying down the weight of my past mistakes and stepping into the fresh start You offer. God, please grant me the courage to release old regrets and to trust that each new beginning is guided by Your loving hand.

Lord, help me to believe that Your timing is perfect—even when my plans feel delayed or uncertain. Teach me patience as I wait for doors to open and for Your purpose to unfold at just the right moment. Help me to rest in the assurance that You make all things beautiful in Your time and that You know what is best for me.

Holy Spirit, align my heart, my choices, my steps, and my plans with God's will. Show me the path You've set before me and keep me aware of Your gentle whisper. May every decision I make reflect Your wisdom, and may I walk in Your purpose for my life each day.

In Jesus Name,

AMEN

Action:

- Identify one area where you need a fresh start and create a plan to change the outcome.
- When impatience or doubt arises, pause and pray, "Lord, I trust Your timing."
- Before making a major choice, ask: "Is this leading me closer to God's purpose for me?"

Affirmation:

"I embrace new beginnings, rest in God's perfect timing, and walk aligned with His will."

Scriptures:

- Lamentations 3:22–23 — "His mercies are new every morning; great is Your faithfulness."
- Ecclesiastes 3:11 — "He has made everything beautiful in its time."
- Proverbs 3:5–6 — "Trust in the Lord with all your heart… He will make your paths straight."

Song: "Blessed Assurance" - CeCe Winans

A Prayer for Trusting God in Transition

Heavenly Father,
I stand at a crossroad of change, my heart conflicted and heavy with both hope and uncertainty. In this season of transition, teach me to release my grip on familiar paths and allow you to lead the way. When reality causes my plans to shift, grant me the courage to pivot—to follow where Your Spirit guides rather than cling to what once was.

Lord Jesus, You embraced divine redirection throughout Your earthly journey, stepping into new callings with bold obedience. As I face decisions that demand me to walk in a different direction, fill me with that same fearless trust. When doubt whispers fear of failure, speak Your truth into my doubt: that "for You, all things are possible," and that "He who began a good work in me will carry it to completion."

Holy Spirit, be my constant guide. In moments of hesitation, nudge me toward the next right step and illuminate the paths that align with God's kingdom. As I learn to pivot with grace, shape my character to reflect resilience, flexibility, and unwavering faith. May my life become a testimony that trusting You through transition isn't merely surviving change but thriving in divine redirection.

In Jesus Name,

AMEN

Action:

- Identify a small area where you feel stuck; find a scripture that fits the theme of what you need to overcome and share your thoughts with a trusted friend or mentor, asking them to pray for God's clear guidance.

Affirmation:
"I embrace God's timing, pivoting with bold faith as He redirects my path for His glory."

Scripture:

- Psalm 32:8 — "I will instruct you and teach you in the way you should go; I will counsel you with my eye upon you."

Song: "Incredible God, Incredible Praise" - JJ Hairston

A Prayer for Spiritual Boldness

Heavenly Father,

You have called me to walk in confidence and steadfast devotion, yet I often find myself shrinking or growing weary. Today, I ask You for a spirit of boldness to proclaim Your truth without fear, and for the discipline to remain faithful in prayer, Scripture, and obedience. Fill me with courage to step beyond my comfort zones and with steadfast resolve to commune with You daily—never relying on my own strength, but on the power of Your Spirit.

Lord Jesus, You modeled both daring love and disciplined devotion—rising early to pray and fast in the wilderness. Teach me to follow Your example: bold in mission and disciplined in communion. When fear whispers lies of inadequacy, remind me that Your grace equips me for every good work. When distractions threaten my devotion, anchor my heart in the joy of Your presence.

Holy Spirit, be the architect of my character. Break lazy habits and replace them with patterns of intentional worship, study, and service. Empower me to advance Your kingdom with fearless faith and to cultivate the habits that sustain a powerful walk with You. May my life testify that true boldness and discipline spring from a heart surrendered to You.

In Jesus Name,

AMEN

Action:

- Each morning, speak aloud one bold prayer request and then spend 10 minutes in Scripture—lean into both courage and consistency.
- Memorize 2 Timothy 1:7 and 1 Corinthians 9:24 – 27; recite them when you feel fear or distraction.

Affirmation:

"I walk in Spirit-enabled boldness and disciplined devotion; God's power sustains every step."

Scriptures:

- 2 Timothy 1:7 — "For God gave us a spirit not of fear but of power and love and self-control."
- 1 Corinthians 9:24 – 27 — "Run in such a way as to get the prize… I discipline my body and keep it under control."

Song: "Yes"-Shekinah Glory Ministry, Valencia Lacy

A Prayer for Peace, Sacred Stillness and Solitude

Heavenly Father,
You are my refuge and strength, a very present help in times of chaos. Today I long for the peace that surpasses all understanding—an inner calm that neither circumstances nor sorrows can shake. Grant me sacred stillness in the quiet of Your presence, where my racing thoughts slow and my restless heart finds rest. Teach me to embrace solitude not as loneliness but as a holy appointment with You, where distractions fall away and I can hear Your gentle whisper guiding my soul.

Jesus, You often withdrew to lonely places to pray (Mark 1:35). In my own wilderness moments, remind me that solitude is a sacred gift—an invitation to pour out my burdens and to drink deeply from the wellspring of Your grace. When the world tugs at me with noise and demands, anchor me in Your peace and lead me into the quiet spaces where You dwell.

Holy Spirit, breathe Your still, small voice into my days. Carve out rhythms of silence and reflection, so that every pause becomes a gateway to deeper communion. May this sacred solitude renew my strength, sharpen my focus on what truly matters, and overflow in compassion for those I serve.

In Your Son Jesus Name,

AMEN

Action:

- Schedule two "Sacred Solitude" slots this week (10–15 minutes): silence phone, find a quiet corner, and simply breathe God's name.
- Practice a two-minute "Peace Pause" whenever you feel overwhelmed: close your eyes, inhale "Lord," exhale "peace."
- Keep a "Solitude Journal": note any insights, Scriptures, or impressions that come during these quiet moments.

Affirmation:

"In God's stillness I find perfect peace; in sacred solitude I renew my soul."

Scriptures:

- Psalm 46:10 — "Be still, and know that I am God."
- Philippians 4:6–7 — "Do not be anxious… and the peace of God… will guard your hearts."
- Mark 6:31 — "Come away by yourselves to a desolate place and rest a while."

Song: "My Life is In Your Hands" - Gods Property

A Prayer for Embracing Grace and Mercy

Heavenly Father,
I come before You aware of my need for Your unmerited favor in this moment of what seems like failure and in season of uncertainty. Your Word reminds me that Your mercies are new every morning (Lamentations 3:22–23), and Your grace is sufficient for every weakness (2 Corinthians 12:9). Today, I open my heart to receive fresh grace: the strength to stand, the courage to hope, and the freedom to live in the beauty of Your forgiveness.

Lord Jesus, You carried my sins on the cross so I might walk unburdened. Teach me to lay down the guilt of yesterday and to embrace the promise of new mercies today. When I stumble, let me run to Your throne of grace and find compassion waiting—never condemnation. Restore my soul with each sunrise and let Your faithful love become the air I breathe.

Holy Spirit, stir within me a profound sense of Your kindness and renewal. In every breath, remind me that I'm not defined by past mistakes but by the fresh work You're doing right now. May Your transforming power shape my thoughts, words, and deeds, that I might extend the same grace to others and shine as a beacon of hope in a world that yearns for mercy.

May my life honor you.
In Jesus Name,

AMEN

Action:

- Begin each morning by whispering, "Your mercies are new for me today," and breathe deeply of God's faithfulness.

- Keep a "Grace Journal": note one way You experienced unearned favor each day.

Affirmation:

"I live every day in the fullness of God's fresh grace and unending mercy."

Scriptures:

- Lamentations 3:22–23 — "Great is your faithfulness; your mercies are new every morning."
- 2 Corinthians 12:9 — "My grace is sufficient for you, for my power is made perfect in weakness.

Song: "Grace and Mercy"-Mississippi Mass Choir

A Prayer for Gratitude and Thankfulness

Heavenly Father,
You have given me the gift of today—its first breath, its rising sun, its unfolding moments.
I come before You awakened and aware that every heartbeat, every smile, every challenge is an invitation to thank You. Teach me to wake each morning with a song of gratitude on my lips, and to carry a grateful heart through every hour that follows. When I rush or grow weary, remind me to pause and offer You thanks—for provision, for presence, and for Your unending mercy that greets me with each dawn.

Lord Jesus, You delight in the simplest acts of thankfulness. Stir in me a spirit that sees Your hand in the ordinary: the kindness of a stranger, the breath of a cool breeze, the warmth of shared laughter. May every breath be a prayer of praise, every step a testimony to Your goodness.

Holy Spirit, be my constant companion in this practice of gratitude. In moments of doubt, whisper reminders of Your faithfulness. In times of abundance, guard me against entitlement. In seasons of lack, open my eyes to Your provision in unexpected places. Let thanksgiving become the soundtrack of my life, so that even my quietest moments echo with praise.

In Jesus Name,

AMEN

Action:

- As soon as you wake up, name aloud three gifts you didn't have yesterday—big or small.

- Set hourly alarms or phone reminders: stop for 30 seconds, take a deep breath, and thank God for whatever comes to mind.

- Before bed, jot down five moments that made you grateful—review them whenever you need to refocus.

Affirmation:

"I wake with thanksgiving and carry gratitude in every moment; God's goodness fills my life."

Scriptures:

- 1 Thessalonians 5:18 — "Give thanks in all circumstances; for this is God's will for you in Christ Jesus."
- Psalm 118:24 — "This is the day that the Lord has made; let us rejoice and be glad in it."

Song: "Grateful" - Hezekiah Walker

Intentional with God

A Prayer for Clarity and Releasing Control

Heavenly Father,
I come with a restless mind and clenched fists, longing for Your clear direction and the freedom that comes when I let go. Grant me spiritual clarity to see Your path through the fog of my fears and desires. Teach me to release my grip on outcomes, trusting that Your wisdom surpasses my understanding and that Your timing is perfect.

Lord Jesus, You surrendered every plan to the Father, stepping out in faith when the road looked uncertain. In my moments of doubt, remind me that true freedom lies in surrender. Replace my anxious striving with the quiet confidence that You hold my future and that every detour is part of Your greater design.

Holy Spirit, illuminate my heart with heavenly insight and soften my desire for control. As I release my own agenda, fill me with courage to follow Your gentle leading. May I walk in holy dependence, anchored in the truth that You guide every step I take.

In Jesus Name,

AMEN

Action:

- Carve out 10 minutes today for a "Clarity Pause": pray, journal what's weighing on you, then breathe out control and listen.
- When anxiety rises about future plans, speak aloud: "Father, I release this outcome into Your hands."
- Track a decision where you feel stuck; prayerfully take the next small step without knowing the full path.

Affirmation:

"I trust God's wisdom over my own, releasing control and walking in His clear direction."

Scriptures:

- Proverbs 3:5–6 — "Trust in the Lord with all your heart… He will make straight your paths."
- Psalm 25:4–5 — "Make me to know Your ways, O Lord; lead me in Your truth… and teach me."
- Philippians 4:6–7 — "Do not be anxious… and the peace of God… will guard your hearts."

Song: "I Surrender All" - CeCe Winans

A Prayer for Hearing God's Voice

Heavenly Father,
In the quiet of my heart I long to be known by You—to have my joys and my sorrows acknowledged by Your loving gaze. Thank You that before I speak a word, You already see me and care for every detail of my life. Open my spiritual ears to your gentle whispers, that I might recognize Your voice above every other sound. Teach me to rest in the assurance that You see my heart and speak truth that guides my steps.

Jesus, You welcomed the outcast and called the lonely by name. In my moments of doubt or insignificance, remind me that I am precious in Your sight (Isaiah 43:1) and that Your voice will never lead me astray (John 10:27). When I feel overlooked by the world, may I hear Your promise: "I have loved you with an everlasting love" and know that I'm fully seen and fully known by You.

Holy Spirit, illuminate my path with Your still, small voice (1 Kings 19:12). Silence the noise of life and prompt me with timely insights and comforting reassurances. May each nudge of Your Spirit draw me deeper into intimacy with God, where I awaken to the truth that I am seen, heard, and deeply loved.

In Jesus Name,

AMEN

Action:

- Today, stop for two minutes—close your eyes, breathe slowly, and whisper, "Lord, I am seen by You."
- Use the Voice Note to record any promptings, scriptures, or impressions you sense from God. Review them nightly for patterns of His guidance.

Affirmation:

"I am fully seen by God; I hear His voice guiding me in love and truth."

Scriptures:

- Psalm 139:1–2 — "O Lord, you have searched me and known me! You know when I sit down and when I rise up."
- John 10:27 — "My sheep hear my voice, and I know them, and they follow me."
- Isaiah 43:1 — "Fear not, for I have redeemed you; I have called you by name, you are mine."

Song: "You Know My Name" -Tasha Cobbs Leonard

A Prayer for Your Relationship with God

Heavenly Father,
Your presence is the heartbeat of my soul, yet I often settle for routine instead of true encounter. Today I long to worship You with all I am—heart, mind, body, and spirit. I often hear your voice, and I ask that you draw me close to you. Teach me that deeper worship isn't about volume or performance, but about the authenticity of a heart laid bare before You.

Lord Jesus, You invited us to abide in You (John 15:4), to dwell moment by moment in Your love. Help me to make intimate communion with You my highest priority—more vital than productivity, more sustaining than any achievement. When distractions pull me away, remind me that nothing compares to the joy of resting in Your presence. Reorder my desires so that seeking You above all else becomes my greatest delight.

Holy Spirit, reignite my hunger and thirst for more of God (Psalm 42:1). Disrupt my complacency and cast light on hidden idols in my heart. Lead me into sacred stillness where I can hear Your voice guiding my steps. As I cultivate rhythms of worship—through prayer, Scripture, silence, and song —transform me from the inside out, making my life a continual act of devotion.

In Jesus Name,

AMEN

Action:

- Challenge yourself to spend 15minutes free of screens and to-dos with God.
- Create a "Praise Journal": after each worship time, write one way you sensed God's presence.
- Fast one meal each week and use that time to pray or listen to God in solitude.

Affirmation:

"I choose deeper worship and place my relationship with God above all else."

Scriptures:

- Matthew 22:37 — "You shall love the Lord your God with all your heart and with all your soul and with all your mind."
- Psalm 27:4 — "One thing have I asked of the Lord… that I may dwell in the house of the Lord all the days of my life."
- John 15:4 — "Abide in me, and I in you. As the branch cannot bear fruit by itself, unless it abides in the vine, neither can you."
- Psalm 42:1 — "As a deer pants for flowing streams, so pants my soul for you, O God."

Song: "As the Deer" - Eddie James

A Prayer for Eliminating Fear and Doubt

Heavenly Father,

You call me to walk by faith and not by sight (2 Corinthians 5:7), yet I often find myself tangled in fear, doubt, and worry. Today, I choose to trust You above my feelings and to step forward on the path You've set before me. Breathe courage into my heart, dispel every anxious thought, and fill me with the peace that surpasses all understanding (Philippians 4:6–7). May my eyes stay fixed on Jesus, my Pioneer and Perfecter of faith (Hebrews 12:2), as I lean not on my own understanding but on Your unfailing wisdom (Proverbs 3:5).

Lord, when fear whispers lies, remind me that You have overcome the world (John 16:33) and that no trial can separate me from Your love.

Holy Spirit, empower me to replace worry with worship, doubt with declaration, and fear with faithful praise. As I walk step by step in faith, may my life become a living testimony of Your strength in my weakness and Your victory over every worry.

In Jesus Name,

AMEN

Action:

- When anxious thoughts arise, pause and say aloud a promise of God (e.g., "God is with me; I will not fear" – Isaiah 41:10).
- Keep a "Faith Journal": note one step of faith you took each day and how God met you.
- Share with a trusted friend one fear you're releasing; pray together and declare victory in Christ.

Affirmation:

"I walk by faith, not by sight; God's perfect peace rules my heart, free from fear, doubt, and worry."

Scriptures:

- 2 Corinthians 5:7 — "For we walk by faith, not by sight."
- Isaiah 41:10 — "Fear not, for I am with you… I will strengthen you and help you."
- Philippians 4:6–7 — "Do not be anxious about anything… and the peace of God will guard your hearts."
- Hebrews 12:2 — "Looking to Jesus, the founder and perfecter of our faith."

Song: "Turning Around for Me" - VaShawn Mitchell

A Prayer for Inviting God In and Centering Joy

Heavenly Father,
I open wide the door of my heart and invite You to move in every corner of my life. Fill this space with Your presence so deeply that joy becomes my constant companion—even when my to-do list and deadlines feel heavy. Teach me to recognize Your hand in simple moments: the laughter of friends, the sunrise in my window, the beat of my favorite song. Let each breath I take be a reminder that true joy springs from knowing I walk with You.

Lord Jesus, You promised that in Your presence there is fullness of joy (Psalm 16:11). When anxiety or exhaustion knocks at my door, remind me to pause, breathe, and lean into You. Replace every worry with worship and every rush with rest, so that through it all, I center my life on the joy You freely give. May Your joy overflow through me, spilling out to uplift everyone I meet.

Holy Spirit, be my guide into the joy that never fades. Stir my soul toward gratitude in every circumstance and guard my heart against bitterness or distraction. Align my thoughts, my words, and my actions with the delight You take in me. As I practice reflection and praise, let me bear the fruit of joy in all I do.

In Jesus Name,

AMEN

Action:

- Before checking phone in the morning, whisper, "Jesus, I invite You into my day," then list three reasons He's already faithful.
- Set a 2-minute reminder to close your eyes, inhale "Joy," exhale "Jesus," and thank Him for a single blessing.
- Create a gratitude jar and drop one note each evening of something that brought you God-filled joy. Watch how Your story stacks up over time.

Affirmation:

"I welcome God's presence and walk in the joy He makes new every morning."

Scriptures:

- Psalm 16:11 — "In Your presence there is fullness of joy; at Your right hand are pleasures forevermore."
- Nehemiah 8:10 — "The joy of the Lord is your strength."
- Zephaniah 3:17 — "He will quiet you with His love; He will rejoice over you with gladness."

Song: "Open My Heart" - Yolanda Adams

A Prayer for Reigniting Your Fire for Christ

Heavenly Father,
My heart once blazed with passion for You, but pride, routine, and the noise of the world have cooled my flame. Today I cry out for a fresh touch—a divine spark to set my spirit ablaze again. Ignite in me holy zeal so every breath and every step becomes a fiery offering of worship.

Lord Jesus, I refuse to be lukewarm. You warned that those who are neither hot nor cold will be spit out (Revelation 3:15–16). Remind me of the gift You placed in me (2 Timothy 1:6). Breathe new life into my devotion, that I might serve with joy, pursue Your presence relentlessly, and run this race with endurance.

Holy Spirit, fall fresh on me like wildfire. Burn away distraction, complacency, and fear. Stir in me a hunger for Your Word, boldness for Your mission, and compassion for Your people. Shape my daily life—prayer, praise, Scripture—into coals that keep my fire glowing.

In Jesus Name,

AMEN

Action:

- Journal three areas where your passion has dimmed and pray over each one.
- Carve out 10 minutes daily to whisper, "Come, Holy Spirit," and simply listen.
- Share your rekindling journey with a friend or small group; pray for one another's fire.

Affirmation:

"My spirit burns bright for Christ; His fire fuels every step I take."

Scriptures:

- 2 Timothy 1:6 — "Fan into flame the gift of God that is in you."
- Revelation 3:15–16 — "Because you are lukewarm… I will spit you out of my mouth."
- Isaiah 40:31 — "Those who hope in the Lord will renew their strength… they shall mount up with wings like eagles."
- Psalm 85:6 — "Will you not revive us again, that your people may rejoice in you?"
- Hebrews 12:29 — "For our God is a consuming fire."

Song: "No Gray"- Johnathan McReynolds

A Prayer for Being Led in Decision Making

Heavenly Father,

I am standing here with so many moving pieces and deadlines pressing in. I confess how easy it is to rush ahead out of fear—fear of missing out, fear of messing up, fear of disappointing. Today, Lord, I choose to pause. I invite You to lead me step by step, whispering Your wisdom and timing over every option on my mind. Teach me to trust YOU more than the ticking clock, knowing that when You direct my steps, I'll never arrive too late or too early.

Jesus, You never flurried through Your calling—you moved in perfect timing and purpose. Remind me that Your plans are never delayed or hurried; they unfold in divine appointed time. When impatience rises, breathe patience into my heart. When doubt creeps in, anchor me with Your assurance that You know the way—even when I can't see the path ahead.

Holy Spirit, be my constant companion in this decision-making season. Calm my racing thoughts, sharpen my spiritual hearing, and align my desires with Your will. Let Your peace guard my heart and mind (Philippians 4:6–7) so that I can move forward with clarity and confidence, supported by Your timing, not driven by my hurry.

In Jesus Name,

AMEN

Action:

- Carve out 5 minutes of silence before making any choice: breathe in "Lead me," breathe out "Your timing."
- Journal the top three options on your heart; pray over each one and make a note which brings lasting peace.
- Ask a trusted friend to pray with you and hold you accountable to wait on God's direction.

Affirmation:

"I walk in God's pace; His timing orders every step I take."

Scriptures:

- Proverbs 3:5–6 — "Trust in the Lord with all your heart… He will make your paths straight."
- Psalm 32:8 — "I will instruct you and teach you in the way you should go; I will counsel you with my eye upon you."
- Isaiah 30:21 — "Whether you turn to the right or to the left, your ears will hear a voice behind you, saying, 'This is the way; walk in it.'"

Song: "They That Wait" - Fred Hammond

A Prayer for Developing the Identity of Christ

Heavenly Father,
You formed me in Your image and redeemed me through Your Son, Jesus. I long to reflect His heart, His love, and His humility in every moment. Shape my thoughts, words, and actions to mirror Christ's character. When pride arises, remind me of His servant-heart. When impatience rises, breathe in His patience. Teach me to walk not by my own understanding but by the Spirit that raised Jesus from the dead.

Lord Jesus, You humbled Yourself and became obedient to the Father, even to the point of the cross. By Your grace, crucify my selfish ambitions and raise up Your compassion, gentleness, and sacrificial love in me. Let my identity rest not in titles or achievements, but in who I am in You—beloved, chosen, and royalty in Your kingdom.

Holy Spirit, fill me with the mind of Christ (1 Corinthians 2:16). Guide me into all truth, convict me where I stray, and empower me to live out my new identity daily. May my heart beat in sync with Yours so that others see Jesus in me and are drawn to You.

In Jesus Name,

AMEN

Action:

- Each morning, choose one Christ-like virtue (e.g., humility, compassion, patience). Ask God to make it alive in you and journal one way you saw it flow out that day.
- Memorize a verse on Christ's character (e.g., Philippians 2:3–8; Colossians 3:12–14). Recite it whenever you face a challenge.
- In conversations and decisions, pause and ask, "What would Jesus do here?" Then take that next obedient step in faith.

Affirmation:

"The character of Christ is being formed in me; I walk daily in His love, humility, and truth."

Scriptures:

- Romans 8:29 — "For those God foreknew he also predestined to be conformed to the image of his Son."
- Ephesians 4:22–24 — "Put off your old self…and put on the new self, created to be like God in true righteousness and holiness."
- Galatians 2:20 — "I have been crucified with Christ and I no longer live, but Christ lives in me."

Song: "Make Me Over" - Tonex, Peculiar People

A Prayer for Divine Protection and Correction

Heavenly Father,
You are my refuge and my stronghold—my safe place in every storm. Today I ask You to surround me with Your hedge of protection, guarding my steps, my mind, and my heart from every attack of the enemy. Shield me under Your wings so that no weapon formed against me prospers.

At the same time, Father, I invite Your gentle correction. Search my heart and reveal any hidden pride, unforgiveness, or wrong paths I'm walking. Refine me through Your discipline, not in anger but in love, so that I emerge stronger, wiser, and more aligned with Your will. When I stray, pull me back; when I doubt, remind me of Your faithful promises.

Holy Spirit, be my guide and protector. Give me eyes to recognize danger, ears to hear Your warnings, and a spirit quick to obey. May Your correction and protection work together in my life, shaping me into the image of Christ and keeping me safe in His name.

In Jesus Name,

AMEN

Action:

- Before you get your day started, pray Psalm 91:1 over yourself—declare, "I dwell in God's shelter; I rest under His wings."
- At midday, pause for two minutes. Ask God to search your heart (Psalm 139:23–24), confess anything He reveals, and thank Him for His loving correction.
- Journal one way you sensed God's protection and one area where He's been refining you. Give thanks for both.

Affirmation:

"I am covered by God's protection and shaped by His loving correction; His grace guards and guides me every day."

Scriptures:

- Psalm 91:1–2 — "Whoever dwells in the shelter of the Most High will rest in the shadow of the Almighty."
- Psalm 139:23–24 — "Search me, God, and know my heart; test me and know my anxious thoughts."
- Hebrews 12:5–6 — "My son, do not make light of the Lord's discipline… God disciplines those he loves."

Song: "No Weapon" - Fred Hammond

Healing the Heart

A Prayer for Forgiving Yourself

Heavenly Father,
I come to You with a heavy heart burdened by resentment—anger I've held onto for too long, guilt I can't shake, and wounds I keep reopening. Today, I ask You to soften my hardness, to untangle the bitterness choking my joy. Help me lay down every grudge, every harsh word, and every self-condemnation at the foot of the cross, trusting that Your perfect justice and mercy can heal what I cannot.

Lord Jesus, You carried our bitterness and bore our shame so we could be free (Isaiah 53:5). Teach me to follow Your example: to forgive those who've wronged me and, most importantly, to forgive myself for mistakes I regret. When I replay past failures or speak words of self-condemnation, remind me of Your finished work—that in Christ I am new every morning (Lamentations 3:22–23) and no sin is too great for Your grace.

Holy Spirit, break the chains of resentment in my mind and heart. Whisper truth into my spirit that I am fully known and fully loved. Fill me with compassion—for others and for myself—so that I can exchange bitterness for peace, anger for understanding, and shame for grace. May Your gentle power root out every seed of unforgiveness and plant a garden of freedom in its place.

In Jesus Name,

AMEN

Action:

- Write down one name or memory that stirs resentment. Pray over it, then tear the paper and let water carry it away—symbolizing release.
- Journal a letter of forgiveness to yourself, listing three ways God's grace met you in past failures. Read it aloud.

Affirmation:

"I release all resentment, extend forgiveness to myself and others, and walk daily in the freedom of Christ's grace.

Scriptures:

- Ephesians 4:31–32 — "Let all bitterness and wrath… be removed…and be kind to one another, tender-hearted, forgiving one another, as God in Christ forgave you."
- Colossians 3:13 — "Bear with one another… and, if one has a complaint against another, forgiving each other; as the Lord has forgiven you, so you also must forgive."

Song: "Take Me to the King" - Tamela Mann

A Prayer for Mending a Broken Heart

Heavenly Father,
My heart is tender from past pain, feeling the ache of what was lost and the fear of loving again. Yet I know You are the Great Healer, the One who binds up the brokenhearted (Psalm 147:3). Today I bring my shattered pieces to You. Pour into me Your gentle comfort, replace my disillusionment with hope, and teach me to rest in Your unfailing love. Remind me that every scar carries a story of Your faithfulness, and that You make all things new.

Jesus, You know what it feels like to be wounded and rejected. As I learn to trust again, infuse me with Your courage. When doubt or fear whispers lies, speak Your truth into my soul: that nothing can separate me from Your love (Romans 8:38–39) and that You will guide me into safe harbors of relationship and intimacy. Help me surrender my control and step forward in faith, confident that You order my steps (Proverbs 3:5–6).

Holy Spirit, be the steady compass of my heart. Soften any walls I've built, break down every barrier of bitterness, and fill me with compassion—for others and for myself. As I open my hands and my heart, renew in me the willingness to trust, to hope, and to love without reservation. May each new connection be a testament to Your redeeming grace.

In Jesus Name,

AMEN

Action:

- Write down one hurt you're still carrying. Pray over it, then tear the paper and release it to God as a symbol of letting go.
- Each day list one small step of trust you took—reaching out, sharing your story, or simply smiling at someone new. Review weekly to see progress.
- Enlist a friend or mentor to pray with you regularly, sharing victories and setbacks as you learn to trust again.

Affirmation:

"I am restored by God's love; I choose to trust again, believing He guides my heart into new hope."

Scriptures:

- Psalm 147:3 — "He heals the brokenhearted and binds up their wounds."
- Romans 8:38–39 — "Nothing can separate us from the love of God in Christ Jesus."
- Proverbs 3:5–6 — "Trust in the Lord with all your heart… He will make straight your paths."

Song: "Alpha and Omega - Live" by Isreal & New Breed

A Prayer for Healing Generational Wounds

Heavenly Father,
You see the echoes of my past—the childhood hurts that still leave scars, the patterns passed down through generations, and the broken trust from relationships that cut deep. I bring every wound to You now. Heal the inner child in me who feels unseen. Break the chains of family pain that have bound my heart. Mend the cracks left by hurtful words, shattered promises, and love that turned to pain. Pour in Your grace so I can walk free, whole, and secure in Your unshakable love.

Lord, You carried our wounds on the cross and bore the weight of generations. By Your stripes, I claim healing for every memory that still wounds me. Teach me to forgive those who hurt me—and myself for holding on too long—so I can release bitterness and step into restoration. Fill me with new trust, new hope, and a new story rooted in Your redemption.

Holy Spirit, Come as Comforter, breaking every stronghold of shame, fear, and resentment. Breathe Your life into the broken places. Stir in me courage to face what I've buried and to celebrate the freedom You've bought. May Your light root out the lies I've believed and plant me in the newness that only You bring.

In Jesus Name,

AMEN

Action:

- Write down one childhood hurt, one generational pattern, and one relationship betrayal. Pray over each, then tear the paper and let God wash you clean.
- List three people (including yourself) you need to forgive. Pray a simple blessing over each name, releasing them into God's hands.
- Share one insight from this prayer with a trusted friend or mentor. Ask them to pray with you and speak truth over your journey.

Affirmation:

"I am a child of God, untangled from past pain, walking in freedom, love, and restored trust."

Scriptures:

- Psalm 147:3 — "He heals the brokenhearted and binds up their wounds."
- Isaiah 61:1 — "He has sent me to bind up the brokenhearted… to proclaim liberty to the captives."
- Ephesians 2:19–20 — "You are no longer strangers… but fellow citizens with God's people."

Song: "Break Every Chain" -Tasha Cobbs Leonard

A Prayer for Self-Love and Self-Compassion

Heavenly Father,
You created me in Your image—fearfully, wonderfully, uniquely made—and yet I've let lies shape how I see myself. I've measured my worth by performance, opinions, and past mistakes. Today I ask You to reveal my true worth: not in what I do, but in who I am in You. Open my eyes to the truth of my identity as Your beloved child, chosen and called for good works (Ephesians 2:10) before the world began. Soften my heart toward myself, teaching me to extend the same gentle compassion You lavish on me, especially when I stumble or feel unworthy. Break every lie that says I'm not enough and fill me with the grace to treat my own heart with the same compassion You show me.

Jesus, help me celebrate my uniqueness, anchor me in the promise that nothing can separate me from Your love, and nothing I face can cancel the worth You've stamped on my soul (Romans 8:38–39).

Holy Spirit, breathe gentleness into my spirit and kindness into my inner dialogue. Break every chain of self-condemnation and replace harsh self-talk with affirmations of truth. Guide me into practices—prayer, reflection, journaling—that cultivate self-compassion. May my identity in Christ become so rooted and sure that I stand firm in every season, confident of my value and careful with my own heart.

In Jesus Name,

AMEN

Action:

- Choose one area where you've judged yourself harshly. Write a letter to yourself from God's perspective, then read it aloud.
- List three things you appreciate about yourself—your character, gifts, or small victories.

Affirmation:

"I am God's masterpiece, beloved and redeemed; I extend to myself the same grace He gives me."

Scriptures:

- Psalm 139:14 — "I praise you because I am fearfully and wonderfully made."
- Ephesians 2:10 — "We are God's handiwork, created for good works."

Song: "God In Me" - Mary Mary and Keirra Clark-Sheard

A Prayer for Breaking Unhealthy Patterns

Heavenly Father,
I come before You weary from cycles that keep repeating—thoughts, habits, and choices that pull me away from Your best for me. I confess the ways I've given in to comfort, distraction, and old ways of coping that no longer serve Your purpose. Today I ask for Your mercy to wash over me and Your strength to shatter every chain that binds me to these patterns.

Lord Jesus, You broke the power of sin and death when You rose from the grave (1 Corinthians 15:57). By Your blood, I claim freedom from behaviors that hold me captive. Renew my mind and transform my heart so that I no longer conform to the patterns of this world but made new in Christ (Romans 12:2; 2 Corinthians 5:17). Teach me to walk in Your Spirit, resisting temptation and choosing life-giving paths.

Holy Spirit, come with Your refining fire. Show me the triggers and thought-loops behind my unhealthy habits. Give me the wisdom to replace them with ways that honor You—moments of silence instead of scrolling, truth instead of lies, healthy boundaries instead of people-pleasing. Empower me day by day to live in the freedom You purchased for me.

In Jesus Name,

AMEN

Action:

- Spend five minutes each morning listing situations or emotions that spark unhealthy patterns.
- For every trigger, choose one godly response (e.g., prayer, Scripture, walk, call a friend).
- Share your goals with someone you trust; check in weekly about wins and setbacks.
- At day's end, write one way you experienced God's freedom—even in small victories.

Affirmation:

"I am free in Christ; each day I walk in newness of life and no pattern has power over me."

Scriptures:

- 2 Corinthians 5:17 — "If anyone is in Christ, he is a new creation. The old has passed away; behold, the new has come."
- Psalm 51:10 — "Create in me a clean heart, O God, and renew a right spirit within me."
- Galatians 5:1 — "For freedom Christ has set us free; stand firm therefore, and do not submit again to a yoke of slavery."

Song: "Cycles (feat. DOE) - Johnathan McReynolds, DOE

A Prayer for Freedom from Shame

Heavenly Father,
I come to You weighed down by the whispers of shame, the voice that tells me I'm not enough. Today, I choose to stand in Your truth instead of hiding in my past hurts. Replace every lie that binds my heart with Your unshakable promises. Remind me that where the Spirit of the Lord is, there is true freedom, and no shame can hold me there.

Lord Jesus, You bore our disgrace on the cross so we could walk in liberty. When memories of failure rise up, help me to run to Your finished work instead of replaying my regrets. By Your grace, strip away every accusation and clothe me in the righteousness You purchased for me. Teach me to gaze at Your wounds and find healing for my own.

Holy Spirit, Fill me with boldness to speak freedom over my life. Break every chain of self-condemnation and breathe life into the places shame once occupied. Lead me into daily habits of confession and celebration—where I confess my brokenness and celebrate Your mercy that washes me clean.

In Jesus Name,

AMEN

Action:

- Each sunrise, declare aloud, "I am no longer defined by shame; Christ's grace sets me free."
- Write down shameful thoughts on paper, then baptize them by safely tearing or burning and praying for release.
- Share one victory over shame with a trusted friend or mentor twice this week.

Affirmation:

"I walk in the freedom Christ won for me; shame has lost its power over my life."

Scriptures:

- Psalm 147:3 — "He heals the brokenhearted and binds up their wounds."
- Romans 8:1 — "There is now no condemnation for those who are in Christ Jesus."

Song: "Where the Spirit Is" - Kirk Franklin & The Family

A Prayer for Softening a Hardened Heart

Heavenly Father,
I come with a heart that feels like stone—worn down by hurt, shielded by anger, and numb to Your voice. Today I ask You to melt away every layer of hardness and replace it with compassion, tenderness, and healing. Pour Your love into the cracks where pain has settled and breathe Your peace into every wound. Teach me to release resentment and to rest in the truth that You are my healer and my Comforter.

Lord Jesus, You endured rejection, betrayal, and agony that no one else could bear. In my moments of bitterness, remind me of Your sacrifice and Your grace that covers every offense. By Your stripes, I claim freedom from the rage and sorrow that bind my spirit. Soften my heart with the same mercy You extended on the cross and help me extend forgiveness to those—and to myself—who have hurt me.

Holy Spirit, break the chains of anger that fuel my defenses. Show me the roots of pain I've buried too deep to face. Pour in Your living water to flush out old wounds and to cultivate a heart of flesh, tender and responsive to love. As You reshape my interior life, empower me to walk in renewed kindness, patience, and self-compassion.

In Jesus Name,

AMEN

Action:

- Spend five minutes journaling the situations or memories that ignite anger.
- Write each painful thought on paper, then tear or burn it as an act of handing it to God.
- List one person (including yourself) you need to forgive; pray a simple blessing over each name.
- When you feel anger rising, pause, breathe deeply, and whisper, “Jesus, heal my heart.”

Affirmation:

“I open to God’s gentle love; my heart grows tender, free from pain and anger.”

Scriptures:

- Ezekiel 36:26 — “I will remove the heart of stone from your flesh and give you a heart of flesh.”
- Psalm 147:3 — “He heals the brokenhearted and binds up their wounds.”

Song: “The Battle Is the Lord’s - Yolanda Adams

A Prayer for Resting in God

Heavenly Father,
I come to You worn out from striving and weighed down by an endless to-do list. My strength is spent, and my faith feels faint. Yet I know You invite the weary to find rest in Your arms (Matthew 11:28). Today, I lay my burdens at Your feet and choose to believe that Your power is made perfect in my weakness (2 Corinthians 12:9). Teach me to lean fully on You, trusting that You will renew my soul and lift me up on eagle's wings (Isaiah 40:31).

Lord Jesus, When doubt creeps in and my spirit grows tired, remind me of Your victory over every storm. You calmed the seas with a word and carried me through the darkest night (Mark 4:39). In my exhaustion, speak peace to my heart and pour out Your rest like living water (John 4:14). Help me to refocus not on what I must do but on who You are—my Refuge, my Strength, my Sustainer.

Holy Spirit, Breathe Your gentle presence into every weary corner of my life. Still the noise of my mind and anchor me in Your truth. Guide me into a Sabbath of soul-rest, where doubt dissolves in praise and fear falls away in worship. May Your quiet power remind me that resting in God isn't passive—it's confident surrender to the One who holds tomorrow.

Thank you, God.
In Jesus Name,

AMEN

Action:

- Pause three times today for a "Rest Break": close your eyes, inhale God's name, exhale your worries.
- Before bed, list three ways you saw God provide rest or strength, anchoring your heart in His faithfulness.

Affirmation:

"I trust God's strength in my weakness; I rest in His faithfulness when I'm tired."

Scriptures:

- Matthew 11:28 — "Come to me, all who labor and are heavy laden, and I will give you rest."
- Isaiah 40:31 — "Those who hope in the Lord will renew their strength; they will soar on wings like eagles."
- 2 Corinthians 12:9 — "My grace is sufficient for you, for my power is made perfect in weakness."

Song: "Praise is What I Do" - William Murphy

A Prayer for Hope After Heartbreak

Heavenly Father,
My heart has been shattered by loss and pain,
yet I cling to You as the source of every new beginning.
In these moments of heartache, breathe Your hope into my soul. Remind me that even when the world feels dark, Your light is—promising restoration, joy, and purpose beyond my wounds.

Lord Jesus, You know the sting of betrayal and the ache of goodbyes. When doubt whispers that I'll never heal, speak truth over my spirit: that by Your grace I am being made new (Isaiah 61:1–3). Teach me to gather each broken piece—my dreams, my trust, my joy—and hand them to You for transformation.
Shape my tomorrow from the ashes of today.

Holy Spirit, Fall fresh on me now as my Helper and Healer. Soften the hardened places within and ignite a longing for holy renewal. Guide my steps as I rebuild—strengthen my faith when I'm weary, steady my hands when I'm afraid, and lead me into the full life You've promised. Make my story of recovery a beacon of hope to others.

In Jesus Name,

AMEN

Action:

- Each sunrise, whisper "God of hope, renew me," then name one new dream You sense Him stirring.
- Write down one moment of grace you experienced each day—no matter how small. Review weekly to see God's faithfulness.
- Reach out to a trusted friend or group and share one way God is rebuilding your heart; pray for one another's restoration.

Affirmation:

"I am rising in hope and strength; God is rebuilding my life from the inside out."

Scriptures:

- Romans 15:13 — "May the God of hope fill you with all joy and peace as you trust in him."
- Isaiah 61:1–3 — "He has sent me to bind up the brokenhearted… to bestow on them a crown of beauty instead of ashes."
- Jeremiah 29:11 — "For I know the plans I have for you… plans to give you hope and a future."

Song: "Goodness of God" - CeCe Winans

A Prayer for Navigation Through Sadness

Heavenly Father,
My soul is heavy and my heart trembles at the weight of loss. Grant me the courage to face the ache instead of numbing it away. When tears blur my vision and sorrow threatens to shut me down, whisper Your strength into my spirit. Help me to sit with my pain, to lean into Your comfort, and to trust that You are with me in every dark moment.

Lord Jesus, You wept at Lazarus's tomb and carried sorrow so I would never carry mine alone. In my loneliness and sadness, remind me that Your heart breaks with mine—and that Your grace is sufficient for every tear. Teach me to lean on Your steadfast love, to pour out my questions before You, and to listen for Your gentle voice guiding me toward healing.

Holy Spirit, Be my companion through this valley of grief. Please be a lamp on the path of raw honesty, lead me into safe spaces where I can share my story, and breathe hope into my wounded heart. Stir in me a holy resilience so that each step I take—however small—moves me closer to peace.

In Jesus Name,

AMEN

Action:

- Once a day write freely for five minutes about your grief—no filters, just truth.
- When sadness wells up, inhale "Jesus," exhale "comfort me." Repeat until your heart steadies.
- Call or meet with one trusted friend or mentor weekly to share where you are and pray for one another.

Affirmation:

"I have courage to feel my grief; God's presence guides me toward healing and hope."

Scriptures:

- Psalm 34:18 — "The Lord is close to the brokenhearted and saves those who are crushed in spirit."
- Isaiah 41:10 — "So do not fear, for I am with you… I will strengthen you and help you."
- 2 Corinthians 1:3–4 — "Praise be to the God… of all comfort, who comforts us in all our troubles."
- 1 Peter 5:7 — "Cast all your anxiety on him, because he cares for you."

Song: "Never Would Have Made It" - Marvin Sapp

A Prayer for Overcoming Fear of Failure

Heavenly Father,
I come weighed down by the whispers that tell me I'm not enough, that my next step will end in defeat. In the hustle of deadlines and expectations, remind me that failure is not a verdict but a lesson on the road to growth. Teach me to see setbacks as springboards, not stumbling blocks, and to believe that every fall can be a fresh chance to rise stronger.

Lord Jesus, You refused to stay in the grave—you turned the worst moment into the greatest victory. When fear of failing creeps into my mind, shine the light of Your triumph over doubt. Help me anchor my worth in who I am in You—beloved, chosen, and called to greatness—rather than in my successes or mistakes.

Holy Spirit, Breathe courage into my heart and replace every anxious thought with Your peace. When uncertainty shakes my confidence, steady my soul with the reminder that You hold my future. Empower me to step forward in faith, knowing that no misstep can derail the destiny You've written for me.

In Jesus Name,

AMEN

Action:

- Write down one area where fear of failure holds you back. Pray over it, asking God to transform that fear into faith.
  When doubt rises, speak aloud a Scripture promise (e.g., "I can do all things through Christ who strengthens me" – Philippians 4:13).
- Share your next big leap with a trusted friend or mentor. Ask them to pray over you and celebrate both wins and lessons.

Affirmation:

"I walk in God's strength; fear of failure has no power over the purpose He's placed in me."

Scriptures:

- Philippians 4:13 — "I can do all things through him who strengthens me."
- Romans 8:31 — "If God is for us, who can be against us?"
- 2 Timothy 1:7 — "For God gave us a spirit not of fear but of power and love and self-control."
- Proverbs 3:5–6 — "Trust in the Lord with all your heart… He will make straight your paths."

Song: "Confidence" - Tasha Cobbs

A Prayer for Releasing Perfectionism

Heavenly Father,

I come weary from striving to measure up by impossible standards. Your Word tells me that Your strength shines brightest in my weakness, yet I cling to a false security in flawless performance. Today, I lay down the burden of perfectionism and ask You to replace it with the freedom of Your grace. Teach me to see my imperfections not as failures, but as fertile ground for Your power to grow.

Lord Jesus, You humbled Yourself to bear our flaws and carried our weaknesses on the cross. In my moments of self-condemnation, remind me that I am perfected in Your righteousness, not in my deeds. Help me exchange anxiety over outcomes for childlike trust in Your loving hands. Show me that true excellence is found in obedience and dependence on You, rather than in a flawless resume.

Holy Spirit, Break the chains of self-criticism and self-condemnation that keep me locked in a cycle of fear. Soften my heart toward myself and others, filling me with compassion instead of comparison. Guide me into habits of self-care—rest, reflection, and rejoicing in small victories. Empower me to extend the same grace to myself that You lavish upon me every morning.

In Jesus Name,

AMEN

Action:

- Each morning, journal one area where perfectionism haunts you and pray for God's perspective on it.
- Share your progress with a trusted friend; ask them to pray for you and celebrate imperfect steps forward.

Affirmation:

"I am God's masterpiece, lovingly crafted in imperfection; His grace equips me to grow each day."

Scriptures:

- Psalm 147:10 — "His pleasure is not in the strength of the horse…but in those who fear him."
- Matthew 11:28 — "Come to me, all who labor and are heavy laden, and I will give you rest."
- Ephesians 2:10 — "For we are his workmanship, created in Christ Jesus for good works."

Song: "Dear God Live" - Smokie Norful

Secret Prayers

A Prayer for Inner Peace

Heavenly Father,

My heart is restless and my mind races with worries that steal my sense. I come to You now, asking for the gift of inner peace—peace that transcends my circumstances and quiets every anxious thought. Speak Your still, small voice over my fear, and hush the storms within me. Remind me that You are my refuge and strength, an ever-present help in trouble, and that in Your presence I can find perfect rest.

Lord Jesus, You promised "Peace I leave with you; my peace I give you. I do not give to you as the world gives" (John 14:27). When life's pressures press in, help me lean into Your promise instead of my own strength. Teach me to cast every burden on You, trusting that You care for me. Fill me with the assurance that Your grace is sufficient and let Your unfailing love be the anchor of my soul.

Holy Spirit, Fall fresh upon me now. Soften my heart and calm my spirit. Breathe Your tranquility into every corner of my being, transforming my chaos into quiet confidence in God's goodness. Lead me into daily rhythms—prayer, Scripture, worship—that cultivate a resting place within me, where Your peace reigns supreme.

In Jesus Name,

AMEN

Action:

- Begin each day with 2 minutes of silent breathing—inhale "Peace," exhale "Jesus."
- Set a mid-day alarm labeled "Be Still" and pause to pray Psalm 46:10 over your heart.

Affirmation:

"I rest in God's peace; His presence calms my mind and guards my heart."

Scriptures:

- John 14:27 — "Peace I leave with you; my peace I give you. I do not give to you as the world gives. Let not your hearts be troubled, neither let them be afraid."
- Philippians 4:6–7 — "Do not be anxious about anything… and the peace of God, which surpasses all understanding, will guard your hearts and your minds in Christ Jesus."
- Isaiah 26:3 — "You will keep in perfect peace those whose minds are steadfast, because they trust in you."
- Psalm 23:1–2 — "The Lord is my shepherd; I shall not want. He makes me lie down in green pastures. He leads me beside still waters."

Song: "Souls Anchored" - Sunday Service Choir

A Prayer for Wisdom and Discernment

Heavenly Father,
You know all things and guide every step I take. I humbly ask You for wisdom that comes from above (James 1:5). Illuminate my mind with Your truth, open my spiritual ears to hear Your voice, and grant me the discernment to distinguish Your will from my own desires. When choices feel overwhelming, remind me to lean not on my understanding but to trust in Your perfect insight (Proverbs 3:5–6).

Lord Jesus, You are the Way, the Truth, and the Life. Teach me to walk in Your footsteps, mirroring Your humility and love in every decision. When I'm tempted to rush or rely on my own strength, speak Your peace into my heart and steady my steps. Shape my character so that I act in alignment with Your purposes and reflect Your heart in all I do.

Holy Spirit,
Brood over my spirit with the gifts of counsel and understanding (Isaiah 11:2). Guide me into all truth, convict me when I stray, and lead me by Your gentle promptings. As I spend time in prayer and Your Word, deepen my sensitivity to Your voice and empower me to choose the path that brings glory to God and blessing to others.

In Jesus Name,

AMEN

Action:

- Begin each morning asking, "Lord, what wisdom do You have for me today?" and jot down impressions.
- When facing a decision, pause and pray Proverbs 2:6—"For the Lord gives wisdom; from his mouth come knowledge and understanding."
- Memorize one verse on wisdom (e.g., James 1:5) and repeat it whenever doubt arises.
- Find an accountability partner to pray through major choices and share what God is saying.

Affirmation:

"I walk in God's wisdom and discernment, led by His Spirit in every decision."

Scriptures:

- James 1:5 — "If any of you lacks wisdom, let him ask God, who gives generously to all without reproach."
- Isaiah 11:2 — "The Spirit of the Lord shall rest upon him, the Spirit of wisdom and understanding."

Song: "Speak to my Heart"- Donnie McClurkin

A Prayer for Overcoming Anxiety and Depression

Heavenly Father,
I come to You weighed down by swirling anxieties and the heaviness of depression. Remind me to cast my cares upon You because You care for me. When fear tightens its grip and worry steals my rest, speak Your peace that surpasses all understanding into my soul.

Jesus, You are my unchanging strength in the midst of life's storms. Sustain me when I feel unstable and lift me from the pit of despair (Hebrews 13:8; Isaiah 33:6). By Your victory, I declare that depression has no final word—Your grace brings renewal and hope (Romans 8:22).

Holy Spirit, Breathe hope into my anxious mind, shine light on my darkness, and anchor me in Your presence. Guide me into daily rhythms of prayer, praise, and rest so that anxiety loses power and depression fades in the warmth of Your love.

In Jesus Name,

AMEN

Action:

- When anxiety rises, stop for three deep breaths—inhale "Peace," exhale "I trust You."
- Write 1 Peter 5:7 and Philippians 4:6–7 on a note; read them aloud whenever worry returns.
- Each evening, list three moments of God's faithfulness—even small ones—and thank Him.
- Share your heart with a trusted friend or mentor weekly; pray together and hold one another up.

Affirmation:

"I cast every burden on the Lord; His peace guards my heart and renews my spirit."

Scriptures:

- 1 Peter 5:7 — "Cast all your anxiety on him because he cares for you".
- Philippians 4:6–7 — "Do not be anxious… and the peace of God will guard your hearts".
- Hebrews 13:8 — "Jesus Christ is the same yesterday, today, and forever".
- Isaiah 33:6 — "You will be… a place of rivers and streams, the strength of salvation".
- Romans 8:22 — "We know that the whole creation has been groaning".

Song: "Open the Eyes of My Heart" - Jordan G. Welch

A Prayer for Releasing Envy, and Jealousy

Heavenly Father,
I confess the ways I've looked at others and measured my worth by their gifts and successes. Today I choose to lay down the heavy burden of comparison, envy, and jealousy at Your feet. Replace the lie that I'm less with the truth that I am fearfully and wonderfully made (Psalm 139:14). Teach me to celebrate others genuinely and to rest in the unique path You've set before me.

Lord Jesus, You refused to compare Yourself to anyone—even though You could have—so that You might love me into freedom. By Your grace, break the chains of jealousy that bind my heart and fill me with contentment (Philippians 4:11–13). Help me to see every person as someone You deeply cherish and to rejoice in their victories as if they were my own.

Holy Spirit, pour out Your peace where envy has taken root. Guard my thoughts when comparison creeps in and prompt me to speak words of gratitude instead. Remind me that true joy arises not from outperforming others, but from walking daily in the fullness of Your love.

In Jesus Name,

AMEN

Action:

- Identify Triggers: Journal three moments today when you felt envy. Offer each one to God in prayer, asking for His perspective.
- Gratitude Pause: Set a timer three times today to stop and list quietly five things you're thankful for—without looking at anyone else.
- Celebrate Out Loud: When you see someone else's success, text, call, or speak a blessing over them immediately.

Affirmation:

"I am free from comparison; I walk in gratitude, trusting God's unique plan for my life."

Scriptures:

- Galatians 6:4–5 — "Let each one test his own work… so that he may have rejoicing in himself alone, and not in another."
- James 3:14–16 — "Where jealousy and selfish ambition exist, there will be disorder and every vile practice."
- Philippians 4:11–13 — "I have learned to be content… I can do all things through Christ who strengthens me."
- 1 Corinthians 13:4 — "Love… does not envy."

Song: "Never Gonna Let Me Down-Live - Jordan G. Welch

A Prayer for Endurance, and Mental Fortitude

Heavenly Father,
Your power is made perfect in my weakness, yet I often rely on my own frail resolve. Today I ask You to pour supernatural strength into my spirit. Fill me with unwavering courage when I face long days, difficult decisions, and the weight of life's pressures. Remind me that every trial is an invitation to lean into You, the Rock who never fails.

Lord Jesus, You walked the earth weary yet steadfast, carrying burdens far heavier than mine. When doubt and exhaustion press in, whisper Your victory over my fears. Teach me to exchange every anxious thought for a declaration of faith, proclaiming, "I can do all things through Christ who strengthens me." May Your triumph become my anthem in moments of mental strain.

Holy Spirit, Breathe resilience into the depths of my mind. Free me from the lies of defeat and replace them with tenacious hope. Guide my inner dialogue so that each thought is aligned with truth and anchored in Your peace. As I cultivate Christlike endurance, empower me to persevere—undaunted, unshaken, unwavering—through every challenge.

In Jesus Name,

AMEN

Action:

- Schedule a 5-minute "Strength Pause" each morning—close your eyes, breathe "Lord, be my strength," and list one way He's faithful.

Affirmation:

- "I stand firm in God's strength; His power sustains my mind, body, and spirit day by day."

Scriptures:

- Isaiah 40:31 — "Those who hope in the Lord will renew their strength; they will soar on wings like eagles."
- 2 Corinthians 12:9 — "My grace is sufficient for you, for my power is made perfect in weakness."
- Ephesians 6:10 — "Be strong in the Lord and in his mighty power."
- Philippians 4:13 — "I can do all things through Christ who strengthens me."

Song: "Worth Fighting For-Live" - Brian Courtney Wilson

A Prayer for Humility

Heavenly Father,
I come before You aware of how often pride creeps into my thoughts, my choices, and my relationships. Today, I ask You to quiet my ego and teach me the beauty of humility—not as weakness, but as strength surrendered to Your will. Help me to see myself clearly: not higher than I ought, nor lower than You've called me, but as Your beloved child, walking in grace.

Lord Jesus, You humbled Yourself to serve, to suffer, and to save. Let Your example shape my heart. When I'm tempted to seek recognition, remind me that greatness is found in serving others. When I feel overlooked, remind me that You see me. Help me to love without condition, to listen without judgment, and to lead without pride.

Holy Spirit, Refine my spirit daily. Strip away comparison, arrogance, and self-righteousness. Replace them with gentleness, patience, and compassion. Let humility be the lens through which I see others—valuing their stories, honoring their worth, and celebrating their victories. May my life reflect the quiet strength of Christ and bring glory to Your name.

In Jesus Name,

AMEN

Action:

- Begin each day with the prayer, "Lord, help me walk humbly today."
- Choose one person daily to affirm or encourage without expecting anything in return.
- Spend 5 minutes in silence each evening, asking God to reveal any prideful thoughts and surrender them.

Affirmation:

"I walk in humility, rooted in God's truth and guided by His grace."

Scriptures:

- Micah 6:8 — "To act justly and to love mercy and to walk humbly with your God."
- James 4:6 — "God opposes the proud but shows favor to the humble."
- Philippians 2:3 — "Do nothing out of selfish ambition… but in humility value others above yourselves."
- Proverbs 11:2 — "With humility comes wisdom."

Song: "He Wants It All" - Forever Jones

A Prayer for Asking for Help and Using Resources

Heavenly Father,
I come to You humbly, recognizing that I cannot do this alone. I've tried to carry the weight, solve the problems, and push through in my own strength—but now I pause to ask for Your help. Teach me that asking is not weakness, but wisdom. You are my Provider, my Counselor, and my Strength. Open my heart to receive Your guidance and to lean on the support You've placed around me.

Lord Jesus, you never hesitated to ask for help—from the Father in prayer, from friends in companionship, and from others in service. Help me to follow Your example. Remove pride and fear that keep me silent. Show me how to use the resources You've already provided—books, mentors, communities, and tools—without shame or hesitation. Let me steward what I have with faith and creativity.

Holy Spirit, whisper clarity into my confusion. Point me toward the right people, the right words, the right steps. Help me discern which resources are aligned with Your truth and which ones I should release. May I never be too proud to ask, too distracted to notice, or too discouraged to try. Fill me with courage to reach out and wisdom to receive.

In Jesus Name,

AMEN

Action:

- Write down one area where you need help. Pray over it, then reach out to someone who can support you.
- List three tools, people, or opportunities already available to you. Ask God how to use them wisely.
- Each morning, ask: "Lord, what help do You want me to receive today?" Then listen.

Affirmation:

"I am not alone; God equips me with help and resources to walk in purpose and peace."

Scriptures:

- Philippians 4:19 — "And my God will supply every need of yours according to his riches in glory in Christ Jesus."
- Proverbs 11:14 — "Where there is no guidance, a people falls, but in an abundance of counselors there is safety."
- Matthew 7:7 — "Ask, and it will be given to you; seek, and you will find; knock, and it will be opened to you."

Song: "God Provides" - Tamela Mann

A Prayer for Practicing Self-Care and Wellness

Heavenly Father,
You are the giver of life, breath, and balance. In a world that demands so much, I pause to honor the sacred responsibility of caring for the vessel You've entrusted to me. Teach me to see self-care not as indulgence, but as stewardship—tending to my body, mind, and spirit so I can serve You and others with clarity and strength. Help me release guilt and embrace rhythms of rest, nourishment, and reflection.

Lord Jesus, You withdrew to quiet places, honored Sabbath, and welcomed stillness. Let me follow Your example. When I feel overwhelmed, remind me that rest is holy. When I neglect my needs, whisper truth: that I am worthy of care, not because of what I do, but because of who I am in You. Help me set boundaries that protect my peace and prioritize wellness without apology.

Holy Spirit, Guide me into habits that restore and renew. Show me how to listen to my body, honor my emotions, and tend to my soul. Lead me to resources, relationships, and routines that align with Your wisdom. May my self-care be an act of worship—an offering of gratitude for the life You've given me.

In Jesus Name,

AMEN

Action:

- Begin each day with a 5-minute check-in: "How is my body? My mind? My spirit?" Then ask, "What do I need today?"
- Schedule one activity that nourishes each part of you—physical (walk, stretch), emotional (journaling, therapy), spiritual (prayer, Scripture).
- Choose one area where you've overextended. Say "no" with grace and "yes" to rest.

Affirmation:

"I honor my body, mind, and spirit as sacred gifts from God; self-care is my act of worship and wisdom."

Scriptures:

- 1 Corinthians 6:19–20 — "Do you not know that your bodies are temples of the Holy Spirit… therefore honor God with your bodies."
- Mark 6:31 — "Come with me by yourselves to a quiet place and get some rest."
- Proverbs 4:23 — "Above all else, guard your heart, for everything you do flows from it."
- Psalm 23:2–3 — "He makes me lie down in green pastures… He restores my soul."

Song: "Imagine Me" - Kirk Franklin

A Prayer for Respecting My Boundaries

Heavenly Father,
You are the God of order, wisdom, and love. Today I ask for Your strength to honor the boundaries You've helped me set boundaries that protect my peace, preserve my purpose, and reflect my worth in You. Teach me to communicate my limits with grace and clarity, and to stand firm without guilt or fear. Help me recognize that boundaries are not walls, but sacred spaces where love, respect, and growth can flourish.

Lord Jesus, You modeled healthy boundaries in Your ministry—stepping away to rest, saying "no" when needed, and staying aligned with the Father's will. Let Your example guide me. When others push past my limits, give me courage to speak truth in love. When I'm tempted to overextend, remind me that honoring my boundaries is an act of stewardship, not selfishness.

Holy Spirit, Be my inner compass. Help me discern when to say "yes" and when to say "no." Remove the fear of disappointing others and replace it with confidence in Your approval. Let my boundaries reflect Your wisdom and protect the calling You've placed on my life. May I also respect the boundaries of others, honoring their space and choices with compassion.

In Jesus Name,

AMEN

Action:

- Write down three boundaries you've set or want to set. Pray over each one and ask God for strength to uphold them.
- Practice saying "no" with kindness and clarity—no apology, just truth.
- When someone shares a boundary with you, respond with "Thank you for sharing that—I respect it."

Affirmation:

"My boundaries are sacred and wise; I honor them with grace and walk in God's peace."

Scriptures:

- Proverbs 4:23 — "Above all else, guard your heart, for everything you do flows from it."
- Galatians 6:5 — "Each one should carry their own load."
- Matthew 5:37 — "Let your 'Yes' be 'Yes,' and your 'No,' 'No.'"
- 1 Corinthians 6:19 — "Your body is a temple of the Holy Spirit… honor God with your body."

Song: "Jesus Be a Fence Around Me (Live) - Fred Hammond, Radical For Christ

A Prayer for Becoming a Good Friend

Heavenly Father,
Thank You for the gift of friendship—a reflection of Your love and grace. I desire to be a friend who uplifts, listens, and walks in truth. Teach me to love without condition, to speak life, and to show up with compassion and consistency. Help me to be the kind of friend who reflects Your heart, not just in words but in action.

Lord Jesus, You called Your disciples friends and laid down Your life for them. Shape my friendships to mirror that kind of sacrificial love. Let my relationships be rooted in honesty, humility, and spiritual encouragement. When conflict arises, give me the courage to seek peace and the grace to forgive. May my friendships be safe spaces where Your presence dwells.

Holy Spirit, Lead me into God-centered connections—friendships that sharpen me, challenge me, and draw me closer to You. Help me discern who to walk closely with and how to nurture those bonds with prayer, patience, and purpose. Let my circle be filled with people who speak truth, pursue righteousness, and celebrate Your goodness together.

In Jesus Name,

AMEN

Action:

- Reflect on your current friendships. Which ones draw you closer to God? Which ones need healing or boundaries?
- Choose one friend to pray with weekly—share joys, struggles, and spiritual goals.
- Send a note, text, or voice message to affirm a friend's growth or remind them of God's love.

Affirmation:

"I am a faithful, grace-filled friend; my relationships reflect God's love and truth."

Scriptures:

- Proverbs 27:17 — "As iron sharpens iron, so one person sharpens another."
- John 15:13 — "Greater love has no one than this: to lay down one's life for one's friends."
- Ecclesiastes 4:9–10 — "Two are better than one… If either of them falls, one can help the other up."
- 1 Thessalonians 5:11 — "Encourage one another and build each other up."

Song: "I Need You to Survive" - Hezekiah Walker, Love Fellowship Choir

A Prayer for Love

Heavenly Father,
You are the source of perfect love—the kind that heals, restores, and never fails. Today, I open my heart to receive and reflect that love. Teach me to love as You do: with patience, kindness, and humility. Strip away envy, pride, and selfishness, and replace them with compassion, grace, and truth. Let my love be a mirror of Your heart—one that honors, uplifts, and perseveres.

Jesus, You showed us love in action—through sacrifice, service, and forgiveness. Help me to embody that same love in my relationships. When I'm tempted to keep score or hold grudges, remind me that love keeps no record of wrongs. Let me rejoice in truth, protect with tenderness, and trust with boldness. May my love be fierce in faith and gentle in spirit.

Holy Spirit, Fill me with divine love that overflows into every corner of my life. Let it guide my words, shape my choices, and soften my heart. Help me to love those who are hard to love, to forgive those who've hurt me, and to cherish those You've placed in my life. May love be my legacy, my language, and my light.

In Jesus Name,

AMEN

Action:

- Write a letter expressing your gratitude for His love and how you want to grow in loving others.
- Choose one intentional act of love each day—kindness, forgiveness, encouragement.
- Reflect on 1 Corinthians 13:4–7 and ask God to help you live it out.

Affirmation:

"I am rooted in God's love; I love with patience, kindness, and truth, and my heart reflects His grace."

Scriptures:

- **1 Corinthians 13:4–7** — "Love is patient, love is kind… It always protects, always trusts, always hopes, always perseveres."
- **Romans 5:5** — "God's love has been poured out into our hearts through the Holy Spirit…"
- **John 15:12** — "My command is this: Love each other as I have loved you."
- **1 John 4:7** — "Let us love one another, for love comes from God."

Song: "Love (Remix)" - Kirk Franklin & The Family

Purpose, Dreams, and Goals

A Prayer for Clarity on Your Calling and Vision

Heavenly Father,
You are the Author of purpose and the Giver of divine assignments. I come to You with a heart that longs to understand the calling You've placed on my life. In the noise of expectations and the fog of uncertainty, speak clearly. Strip away distractions, doubts, and comparisons so I can hear Your voice above all others. Illuminate the vision You've written into my spirit—one that aligns with Your kingdom, honors my gifts, and serves others with love.

Lord Jesus, You walked with clarity, knowing Your mission and moving with intention. Teach me to walk in that same confidence. When I feel unqualified or overwhelmed, remind me that You chose me before I was formed (Jeremiah 1:5). Help me to trust that the vision You've given is not too big, too late, or too far away. Let me move forward with boldness,
knowing that You go before me.

Holy Spirit, be my compass and my confirmation. Stir up divine ideas, dreams, and direction. Reveal the next step, even if it's small. Let Your peace be my guide and Your conviction be my anchor. Surround me with wise counsel and open doors that no one can shut. May my calling be clear, my vision be focused, and my heart be surrendered to Your will.

In Jesus Name,

AMEN

Action:

- Write down what stirs your spirit—dreams, ideas, burdens. Ask God to highlight what's from Him.
- Read Jeremiah 29:11 and Isaiah 30:21 daily for one week. Listen for God's whisper.
- Take a walk in silence, asking God to speak through nature, thoughts, or impressions.

Affirmation:

"I am called by God, equipped for purpose, and guided by divine vision. I walk boldly in clarity and faith."

Scriptures:

- Jeremiah 1:5 — "Before I formed you in the womb I knew you, before you were born I set you apart."
- Isaiah 30:21 — "Whether you turn to the right or to the left, your ears will hear a voice behind you, saying, 'This is the way; walk in it.'"
- Proverbs 29:18 — "Where there is no vision, the people perish."

Song: "Make Room" - Jonathan McReynolds

A Prayer for Releasing Imposter Syndrome

Heavenly Father,
I come to You burdened by the weight of self-doubt and delay. I've questioned my worth, second-guessed my calling, and postponed the very things You've placed in my hands. Today, I surrender the fear that whispers "I'm not enough" and the hesitation that keeps me stuck. Remind me that I am chosen, equipped, and empowered by Your Spirit—not by perfection, but by grace.

Lord Jesus, You never needed credentials to walk in purpose. You simply obeyed. Help me do the same. When imposter syndrome tells me I'm a fraud, speak louder with Your truth: that I am Your workmanship, created for good works (Ephesians 2:10). When procrastination tempts me to wait for the "perfect moment," remind me that obedience is better than delay and that Your timing is now.

Holy Spirit, Break the cycle of comparison and fear. Stir up boldness in me to act, even when I feel unsure. Replace paralysis with progress, and hesitation with holy momentum. Guide me to use the gifts You've given—not flawlessly, but faithfully. Let me walk in confidence, not because I have it all together, but because You go before me.

Thank You God for My Life.
In Jesus Name,

AMEN

Action:

- Each morning, look in the mirror and declare: "I am called, capable, and covered by grace."
- Write down one task you've delayed. Take one small step today, then celebrate the progress.
- Set a daily reminder that says: "I am not an imposter—I am God's masterpiece in motion."

Affirmation:

"I release fear and delay; I walk boldly in my calling, trusting God's grace over my perfection."

Scriptures:

- Ephesians 2:10 — "We are God's handiwork, created in Christ Jesus to do good works…"
- 2 Timothy 1:7 — "God gave us a spirit not of fear but of power and love and self-control."
- Philippians 1:6 — "He who began a good work in you will carry it on to completion…"

Song: "The Best In Me" - Marvin Sapp

A Prayer for Trusting the Process

Heavenly Father,
You are the Author of time and the Architect of every season. When the path feels slow, uncertain, or winding, remind me that You are never late. Teach me to trust the process—not just the destination—and to believe that every delay, detour, and quiet moment is part of Your divine design. Help me release the need to control outcomes and instead rest in Your perfect timing.

Jesus, You waited thirty years before stepping into Your public calling. You knew the value of preparation, of hidden seasons, of quiet obedience. When I feel behind or overlooked, remind me that You are preparing me for something greater than I can see. Let me walk with patience, knowing that the process is not punishment—it's refinement.

Holy Spirit, Be my steady guide when impatience creeps in. Whisper peace when I want to rush ahead. Help me embrace the slow work of transformation, trusting that You are shaping me in the waiting. Let my heart be anchored in faith, not fear. May I find joy in the journey, knowing that You are with me in every step.

In Jesus Name,

AMEN

Action:

- Write down one area of your life where you feel stuck or impatient. Ask God to show you what He's doing beneath the surface.
- Read Isaiah 40:31 each morning and reflect on what it means to "renew your strength."
- At the end of each day, list one thing you're thankful for in the process—even if it's small.

Affirmation:

"I trust God's timing and embrace the process; patience is growing in me day by day."

Scriptures:

- Isaiah 40:31 — "But those who wait for the Lord shall renew their strength…"
- Ecclesiastes 3:1 — "There is a time for everything, and a season for every activity under the heavens."
- Romans 8:28 — "And we know that in all things God works for the good of those who love him…"
- James 1:4 — "Let perseverance finish its work so that you may be mature and complete, not lacking anything."

Song: "They That Wait" - Fred Hammond, John P. Kee

A Prayer for Commitment and Discipline

Heavenly Father,
You are the God of beginnings and completions—the Alpha and the Omega. You've placed dreams, goals, and vision within me, and I thank You for the fire of ambition that stirs my spirit. But I ask now for Your wisdom to balance that drive with grace, rest, and discernment. Teach me to pursue excellence without idolizing achievement. Help me to honor the process, not just the outcome, and to walk in purpose without rushing ahead of Your timing.

Lord Jesus, You finished the work the Father gave You, not with haste but with holy intention. When I feel overwhelmed or tempted to quit, remind me that You are my strength. Help me to finish what I start—not for applause, but for obedience. Let my ambition be rooted in service, not self. When distractions or discouragement arise, anchor me in Your example of perseverance and peace.

Holy Spirit, guide me in setting healthy routines—of work and rest, of dreaming and doing. Show me when to pause, when to push, and when to release. Fill me with clarity to prioritize what matters and courage to complete what I've begun. Let my ambition be sanctified by surrender, and my follow-through be fueled by faith.

In Jesus Name,

AMEN

Action:

- Write down your top three ambitions. Ask: "Do these align with God's will and timing?"
- Choose one unfinished task this week and commit to completing it with prayer and intention.
- Schedule one hour of rest or reflection for every two hours of focused work. Invite God into both.

Affirmation:

"I pursue purpose with peace; I finish what I start through God's strength and grace."

Scriptures:

- Philippians 1:6 — "He who began a good work in you will carry it on to completion…"
- Ecclesiastes 3:1 — "There is a time for everything, and a season for every activity under the heavens."
- 2 Timothy 4:7 — "I have fought the good fight, I have finished the race, I have kept the faith."

Song: "Encourage Yourself" - Sheri Jones-Moffett

A Prayer for Eliminating Distractions

Heavenly Father,
In a world overflowing with noise, I come seeking Your stillness. My mind is pulled in a thousand directions—by screens, schedules, and self-doubt. Today, I ask You to quiet the chaos and help me focus on what truly matters. Teach me to guard my attention like a sacred gift, and to center my thoughts on Your truth, Your presence, and Your purpose.

Lord Jesus, You withdrew to quiet places to pray, showing us the power of intentional focus. Help me follow Your example. When distractions rise, remind me that clarity begins with surrender. Let me not be swayed by urgency or comparison but anchored in Your peace. Give me discernment to recognize what is pulling me away from You—and the courage to release it.

Holy Spirit, Be my filter and my focus. Guide my eyes, my ears, and my heart toward what is life-giving. Help me create rhythms of silence, prayer, and reflection that restore my soul. Let every moment be an invitation to return to You. May I walk through each day with intention,
choosing presence over pressure
and purpose over performance.

In Jesus Name,

AMEN

Action:

- Choose one hour each day to unplug from devices and spend time in prayer, journaling, or quiet reflection.
- Write down Philippians 4:8 and place it where you'll see it often—let it guide your thoughts.
- List your top three distractions. Pray over each one and ask God how to shift your habits.
- Set a timer three times a day to stop, breathe deeply, and whisper, "Lord, refocus me."

Affirmation:

"I release distractions and embrace divine focus; my mind is anchored in peace and purpose."

Scriptures:

- Philippians 4:8 — "Whatever is true, whatever is noble… think about such things."
- Proverbs 4:25–27 — "Let your eyes look straight ahead… do not turn to the right or the left."
- Isaiah 26:3 — "You will keep in perfect peace those whose minds are steadfast, because they trust in you."
- Psalm 46:10 — "Be still, and know that I am God."

Song: "You're Bigger" - Jekalyn Carr

A Prayer for Redefining Success

Heavenly Father,
In a world that measures success by status, wealth, and applause, I pause to ask You to redefine what success means in my life. Strip away every false metric and comparison that clouds my vision. Teach me that true success is found in obedience, integrity, and love. Help me to pursue purpose over popularity, impact over image, and faithfulness over fame.

Lord Jesus, You walked humbly, served quietly, and fulfilled Your mission without seeking worldly validation. Let Your example guide me as I grow. When ambition tempts me to compromise, anchor me in authenticity. Remind me that I don't have to perform to be worthy—I am already chosen, called, and loved. Help me to build with intention, not imitation.

Holy Spirit, be my compass in every season of growth. Whisper truth when I feel pressure to conform. Empower me to stay rooted in who You created me to be, even as I stretch into new spaces. Let my journey be marked by grace, not hustle; by alignment, not striving. May my growth reflect Your glory, not just my goals.

In Jesus Name,

AMEN

Action:

- Each week, journal one way you stayed true to yourself and one area where you felt tempted to perform.
- Write your personal definition of success based on Scripture and purpose. Revisit it monthly.
- Reflect on Micah 6:8 and Colossians 3:23 to realign your heart with God's vision of success.

Affirmation:

"I grow with grace and authenticity; success is obedience to God's call, not the world's applause."

Scriptures:

- Micah 6:8 — "He has shown you… what is good. And what does the Lord require of you? To act justly, love mercy, and walk humbly with your God."
- Colossians 3:23 — "Whatever you do, work at it with all your heart, as working for the Lord…"

Song: "Victory-Live" - Tye Tribbett & G.A.

A Prayer to Embrace Who I Am Becoming

Heavenly Father,
You are the Author of my story, the One who sees the end from the beginning. I surrender my plans, my timeline, and my expectations to You. Even when the path feels uncertain, I choose to trust that Your plans are good, purposeful, and filled with hope (Jeremiah 29:11). Help me release control and lean into Your divine wisdom, knowing that You are shaping me into someone who reflects Your heart.

Lord Jesus, You gave up heaven's glory to walk among us, showing us what it means to live with purpose and humility. Teach me to embrace the identity You've given me—not one shaped by fear, comparison, or past mistakes, but one rooted in grace, truth, and love. Remind me that I am chosen, called, and becoming more like You each day. When I feel lost or unsure, anchor me in the truth that I am Yours.

Holy Spirit, breathe fresh vision into my soul. Reveal the beauty of who I am becoming—not just in what I do, but in how I love, serve, and grow. Help me to walk boldly in my calling, even when I feel unqualified. Let Your voice be louder than doubt, and Your peace be stronger than pressure. Shape my character, refine my gifts, and guide me into the fullness of who You created me to be.

In Jesus Name,

AMEN

Action:

- Write down three truths about who God says you are (e.g., beloved, chosen, redeemed). Revisit them daily.
- Reflect on Ephesians 2:10 and Isaiah 43:19. Ask God to show you what He's building in you.

Affirmation:

"I am becoming who God designed me to be—rooted in grace, led by purpose, and shaped by divine love."

Scriptures:

- Jeremiah 29:11 — "For I know the plans I have for you… plans to give you hope and a future."
- Ephesians 2:10 — "For we are God's masterpiece… created to do good works."
- Isaiah 43:19 — "See, I am doing a new thing! Now it springs up; do you not perceive it?"

Song: "I Give Myself Away" - William McDowell

A Prayer for God-Centered Goals

Heavenly Father,
You are the source of all wisdom, purpose, and direction. Today I surrender my ambitions to You—not to be diminished, but to be refined. Align my goals with Your heart, so that what I pursue reflects Your kingdom, not just my desires. Help me to dream boldly, but walk humbly, trusting that Your plans are far greater than anything I could imagine (Jeremiah 29:11).

Lord Jesus, You lived with intention, never distracted by applause or comparison. Teach me to set goals that serve others, honor You, and stretch me toward growth. When I feel pressure to chase success for validation, remind me that true fulfillment comes from obedience. Let my goals be rooted in love, not ego—in service, not selfish gain.

Holy Spirit, Guide my steps with clarity and conviction. Reveal which goals are from You and which ones I need to release. Help me steward my time, energy, and gifts with discipline and joy. Surround me with wise counsel and divine opportunities. May every milestone be marked by grace, and every setback be a setup for deeper trust.

In Jesus Name,

AMEN

Action:

- Write down your top three goals. Ask: "Do these reflect God's heart and purpose for my life?"
- Choose one verse (e.g., Proverbs 16:3) to pray over your goals daily.
- At the start of each month, ask God: "What do You want me to focus on right now?"
- Share your goals with someone who can pray with you and hold you accountable.

Affirmation:

"My goals are rooted in God's purpose; I pursue them with faith, wisdom, and grace."

Scriptures:

- Proverbs 16:3 — "Commit to the Lord whatever you do, and He will establish your plans."
- Colossians 3:23 — "Whatever you do, work at it with all your heart, as working for the Lord…"
- James 1:5 — "If any of you lacks wisdom, let him ask God… and it will be given to him."
- Psalm 37:4–5 — "Delight yourself in the Lord… Commit your way to the Lord; trust in Him…"

Song: "Look At God" - Koryn Hawthorne

A Prayer for Servant Leadership

Heavenly Father,
You are the ultimate example of leadership—one who leads with love, humility, and sacrifice. Today, I ask You to shape my heart into that of a servant leader. Strip away any desire for control, recognition, or status, and replace it with a longing to serve others with grace and wisdom. Teach me to lead not from ego, but from empathy; not for applause, but for impact.

Lord Jesus, You washed feet, welcomed the forgotten, and laid down Your life for those You loved. Let Your example guide my every decision. When I'm tempted to lead from pride, remind me that greatness is found in humility. Help me to listen more than I speak, to uplift more than I direct, and to build others up even when it costs me comfort.

Holy Spirit, empower me to lead with discernment, compassion, and courage. Let my leadership reflect Your fruit—love, joy, peace, patience, kindness, goodness, faithfulness, gentleness, and self-control. Show me how to steward influence with integrity and to create spaces where others feel seen, valued, and inspired. May my leadership always point back to You.

In Jesus Name,

AMEN

Action:

- Ask, “Who did I serve today?” and “Did I lead with humility?”
- In every meeting or conversation, commit to listening fully before responding.
- Choose one person each day to affirm, uplift, or support in their journey.

Affirmation:

“I lead with humility, serve with love, and reflect God’s heart in every decision I make.”

Scriptures:

- Philippians 2:3–4 — “Do nothing out of selfish ambition… but in humility value others above yourselves.”
- Mark 10:45 — “For even the Son of Man did not come to be served, but to serve…”
- 1 Peter 5:2–3 — “Be shepherds… eager to serve… being examples to the flock.”
- Galatians 5:22–23 — “The fruit of the Spirit is love, joy, peace… self-control.”

Song: “I’ve Got My Mine Made Up” - Norman Hutchins

A Prayer for Community Over Competition

Heavenly Father,
You are the God of unity, grace, and abundance. Today I release the need to compete and compare, and I ask You to cultivate a spirit of community within me. Teach me to see others not as rivals, but as reflections of Your creativity and purpose. Help me to celebrate their wins, honor their gifts, and trust that there is room for all of us to thrive.

Lord Jesus, You walked among people with compassion, not competition. You uplifted others, shared wisdom freely, and never withheld love. Let me follow Your example. When envy tries to creep in, remind me that my lane is sacred and my timing is divine. Bless those I once saw as competitors—may their work flourish, their hearts be full, and their impact be great.

Holy Spirit, renew my mindset. Replace scarcity with abundance, comparison with confidence, and rivalry with relationship. Show me how to collaborate, support, and build bridges. Let my presence in any space be one of peace, encouragement, and generosity. May I be known not for striving, but for serving.

In Jesus Name,

AMEN

Action:

- Choose one person or brand you admire and pray for their success. Send a note of encouragement or share their work.
- Host or join a gathering that fosters collaboration—whether a workshop, writing circle, or prayer group.

Affirmation:

"I am rooted in community, not competition. There is space for me and for others. We rise together. I bless others freely, knowing God's abundance covers us all."

Scriptures:

- Philippians 2:3 — "Do nothing out of selfish ambition… but in humility value others above yourselves."
- Galatians 6:4 — "Each one should test their own actions… without comparing themselves to someone else."
- Proverbs 11:25 — "A generous person will prosper; whoever refreshes others will be refreshed."

Song: "Alpha and Omega" - Isreal & New Breed

A Prayer for Celebrating Big and Small Wins

Heavenly Father,
Thank You for every victory—both the ones that made headlines in my heart and the quiet ones that only You and I noticed. You are the Giver of every good thing, and I pause to honor Your hand in my progress. Whether it was a major breakthrough or a moment of courage to keep going, I celebrate it all as evidence of Your faithfulness. Teach me to rejoice not just in the destination, but in every step of the journey.

Jesus, You never overlooked the small moments. You celebrated faith, obedience, and transformation—even when it came in whispers. Help me to do the same. When I'm tempted to wait for the "big win" before I praise, remind me that every act of growth, every answered prayer, and every step forward is worthy of celebration. Let my gratitude be loud, my joy be contagious, and my heart be anchored in You.

Holy Spirit, fill me with a spirit of celebration. Help me to recognize the wins in my relationships, my healing, my creativity, and my faith. Let me be someone who cheers for others, honors progress and gives thanks in all things. May my life be a one of praise—dancing between milestones and miracles, between small steps and giant leaps.

In Jesus Name,

AMEN

Action:

- Write down one big win and one small win each week. Reflect on how God showed up in both.
- At the end of each day, whisper "Thank You" for one moment of progress, no matter how small.
- Send a message or prayer of encouragement to someone who's growing—big or small.

Affirmation:

"I celebrate every win with joy and gratitude; God is present in every step of my journey."

Scriptures:

- Psalm 126:3 — "The Lord has done great things for us, and we are filled with joy."
- Zechariah 4:10 — "Do not despise these small beginnings, for the Lord rejoices to see the work begin."
- 1 Thessalonians 5:18 — "Give thanks in all circumstances…"
- Philippians 1:6 — "He who began a good work in you will carry it on to completion…"

Song: "Total Praise" - Richard Smallwood, Vision

A Prayer for Time Management

Heavenly Father,
You are the Creator of time and the Keeper of seasons. I come to You with a heart that longs for order, clarity, and purpose. In the midst of busy schedules and endless to-do lists, help me to steward my time wisely. Teach me to prioritize what matters most—Your presence, my purpose, and the people You've placed in my life. Let me not be ruled by urgency but guided by intentionality.

Lord Jesus, You moved with purpose and peace, never rushed yet always effective. Help me to follow Your example. When I feel overwhelmed, remind me that You are my strength. When I'm tempted to procrastinate or overextend, whisper Your wisdom into my spirit. Let my time reflect Your grace—not just in productivity, but in rest, reflection, and renewal.

Holy Spirit, be my daily planner. Show me what to say yes to and what to release. Help me to create healthy routines that honor my body, mind, and spirit. Remove distractions and fill my day with divine focus. May every hour be an offering, every task a testimony, and every pause a moment to reconnect with You.

In Jesus Name,

AMEN

Action:

- Begin each day by asking, "Lord, what do You want me to focus on today?"
- Track how you spend your time for three days. Pray over the patterns and ask God to reveal what needs shifting.
- Choose one day or evening each week to unplug, rest, and reflect with God.

Affirmation:

"I steward my time with wisdom and grace; each moment is a gift from God."

Scriptures:

- Ephesians 5:15–16 — "Be very careful, then, how you live… making the most of every opportunity."
- Psalm 90:12 — "Teach us to number our days, that we may gain a heart of wisdom."
- Proverbs 16:3 — "Commit to the Lord whatever you do, and He will establish your plans."
- Colossians 3:23 — "Whatever you do, work at it with all your heart, as working for the Lord…"

Song: "Intentional" - Travis Greene

A Prayer for Wise Financial Stewardship

Heavenly Father,
You are the God of increase, the One who enlarges borders and multiplies blessings. Today I ask You to expand the territory You've entrusted to me—not just in influence or opportunity, but in impact for Your kingdom. Remove every limitation, fear, and barrier that keeps me small. Like Jabez, I boldly pray: "Bless me indeed and enlarge my territory" (1 Chronicles 4:10). Let Your hand be with me, guiding every step as I walk into new spaces with courage and grace.

Lord Jesus, You taught us to be faithful with little so we could be trusted with much. As You expand my reach, teach me to steward every resource—time, money, relationships—with wisdom and integrity. Help me to manage increase without losing sight of You. Let my financial decisions reflect Your values: generosity, discipline, and purpose. May I never chase wealth but always pursue Your will.

Holy Spirit, whisper strategy into my spirit. Show me how to build, invest, and grow with divine insight. Lead me to opportunities that align with my calling and protect me from distractions that dilute my purpose. Let my expansion be marked by peace, not pressure; by stewardship, not striving. May every new door be a testimony of Your favor and every financial choice be an act of worship.

In Jesus Name,

AMEN

Action:

- Write down areas where you desire expansion—business, ministry, influence. Pray over each one and ask God for clarity.
- Reflect on Proverbs 3:9–10 and Luke 16:10 to align your heart with God's principles.

Affirmation:

"I walk in divine expansion and steward every blessing with wisdom, grace, and purpose."

Scriptures:

- 1 Chronicles 4:10 — "Oh, that You would bless me and enlarge my territory…"
- Proverbs 3:9–10 — "Honor the Lord with your wealth… then your barns will be filled…"
- Luke 16:10 — "Whoever can be trusted with very little can also be trusted with much."

Song: "Bless Me (The Prayer of Jabez)" - Donald Lawrence & The Tri-City Singers

The Days Ahead

A Prayer for Future Generations

Heavenly Father,
You are the God of Abraham, Isaac, and Jacob—the God of generations. Today, I lift up those who will come after me: children, grandchildren, and descendants I may never meet. I ask You to cover them with Your grace, wisdom, and protection. May they walk in truth, live with purpose, and carry the torch of faith boldly into the future.

Lord Jesus, You prayed for those who would believe through the testimony of others (John 17:20). I echo that prayer now. Let future generations know You intimately—not just through tradition, but through personal encounter. May they hunger for Your Word, stand firm in righteousness, and be bold witnesses of Your love in a world that desperately needs it.

Holy Spirit, plant seeds of revival in their hearts. Break every generational curse and replace it with generational blessing. Let their lives overflow with creativity, compassion, and conviction. Raise up leaders, healers, artists, and prophets who will shape culture with Kingdom values. May they be known not by fame, but by faithfulness.

In Jesus Name,

AMEN

Action:

- Write a letter or prayer to your future descendants. Share your faith, your story, and your hopes for them.
- Speak blessings aloud over your children or community weekly—declare identity, purpose, and protection.
- Invest in something that will outlive you—mentorship, creative work, or community service that builds legacy.

Affirmation:

"I sow seeds of faith today that will bloom in generations to come. My legacy is rooted in God's love and truth."

Scriptures:

- Psalm 78:4 — "We will not hide them from their children, but tell to the coming generation the glorious deeds of the Lord…"
- Deuteronomy 7:9 — "He keeps His covenant and mercy to a thousand generations…"
- Isaiah 59:21 — "My Spirit… will not depart from your mouth… nor from your descendants…"

Song: "Why We Sing-Live" - Kirk Franklin

A Prayer for Being a Good Spouse

Heavenly Father,
Thank you for the sacred gift of marriage and the calling to love deeply and faithfully. Today, I ask You to shape me into a spouse who reflects Your heart—one who listens with compassion, speaks with kindness, and serves with humility. Help me to honor my partner not just in moments of ease, but especially in seasons of challenge. Teach me to love unconditionally, forgive quickly, and support consistently.

Lord Jesus, You laid down Your life for the Church, showing us the depth of true love. Let Your example guide my actions. When I'm tempted to be selfish or impatient, remind me that love is a choice—a daily commitment to grace and growth. Help me to be present, to nurture connection, and to build a home where peace and joy dwell. May my words uplift and my actions affirm the covenant we share.

Holy Spirit, fill me with wisdom to navigate conflict, tenderness to heal wounds, and strength to remain faithful. Let my marriage be a reflection of Your unity and love. Empower me to be a safe place for my spouse—a source of encouragement, laughter, and spiritual partnership. Shape me into someone who loves well, leads with integrity, and grows in grace.

In Jesus Name,

AMEN

Action:

- Speak one word of affirmation or encouragement to your spouse each day.
- Set aside time weekly to pray together, even if just for five minutes.
- Ask your spouse what makes them feel most loved—and do it intentionally.

Affirmation:

"I am a loving, faithful, and grace-filled spouse; my marriage reflects God's heart and grows stronger each day."

Scriptures:

- Ephesians 5:25 — "Husbands, love your wives, just as Christ loved the church and gave himself up for her."
- Proverbs 31:11–12 — "Her husband has full confidence in her… She brings him good, not harm, all the days of her life."
- Ecclesiastes 4:9–10 — "Two are better than one… If either of them falls down, one can help the other up."

Song: "My Hands Are Lifted Up" - Jovanta Patton

A Prayer for Being a Good Neighbor

Heavenly Father,

Thank You for placing me in a community where I can reflect Your love through everyday interactions. Help me to be a neighbor who listens, serves, and uplifts. Teach me to see those around me not as strangers, but as fellow image-bearers of Your grace. Let my presence bring peace, kindness, and light to the spaces I inhabit.

Lord Jesus, You taught us to love our neighbors as ourselves. You welcomed the outcast, shared meals with the overlooked, and extended compassion to all. Shape my heart to do the same. When I'm tempted to isolate or ignore, stir me to engage with empathy. Help me to offer a smile, a helping hand, or a word of encouragement—small acts that carry eternal weight.

Holy Spirit, guide my steps and conversations. Show me how to build bridges, not walls. Let my home be a place of warmth and welcome, and my words be seasoned with grace. Help me to be attentive to the needs of those around me—whether physical, emotional, or spiritual. May I be a vessel of Your love, creating community wherever I go.

In Jesus Name,

AMEN

Action:

- Write a short note or text to a neighbor expressing appreciation or offering help.
- Walk through your neighborhood and pray silently for each home you pass.
- Do one unexpected act of kindness for a neighbor this week—no strings attached.

Affirmation:

"I am a light in my neighborhood; I love, serve, and build community with grace and intention."

Scriptures:

- Mark 12:31 — "Love your neighbor as yourself."
- Romans 12:10 — "Be devoted to one another in love. Honor one another above yourselves."
- Galatians 5:14 — "The entire law is fulfilled in keeping this one command: 'Love your neighbor as yourself.'"
- Proverbs 3:27 — "Do not withhold good from those to whom it is due, when it is in your power to act."

Song: "Bless Me" - Maverick City Music, Kirk Franklin

A Prayer to Look After Those in Need

Heavenly Father,
You are the Defender of the vulnerable and the Provider for every soul in need. Today, I lift up those who are hungry, hurting, homeless, and forgotten. Wrap them in Your mercy and meet them in their place of lack with Your abundance. Stir our hearts to be Your hands and feet—serving, giving, and loving without hesitation.

Lord Jesus, You walked among the poor, healed the broken, and welcomed the outcast. Let Your compassion flow through me. Help me to see the needs around me and respond with generosity and grace. May I never turn away from suffering but instead lean in with empathy and action. Teach me to love my neighbor as myself, and to honor You by caring for the least of these.

Holy Spirit, ignite a fire of compassion within me. Guide me to those who need encouragement, support, or simply someone to listen. Show me how to use my resources—time, finances, talents—for the good of others. Let my life be a reflection of Your justice, mercy, and love. May I be a vessel of hope in a world that desperately needs healing.

In Jesus Name,

AMEN

Action:

- Write down one person or group in need you've encountered this week. Pray for them and ask God how you can help.
- Choose one act of service each week—volunteering, donating, or simply checking in on someone who's struggling.
- Gather with others monthly to pray for those in need and brainstorm ways to support your community.

Affirmation:

"I am a vessel of compassion; I care for those in need with love, dignity, and purpose."

Scriptures:

- Proverbs 19:17 — "Whoever is kind to the poor lends to the Lord, and He will reward them for what they have done."
- Isaiah 58:10 — "If you spend yourselves in behalf of the hungry… your light will rise in the darkness."
- Matthew 25:40 — "Whatever you did for one of the least of these… you did for Me."
- Psalm 82:3–4 — "Defend the weak and the fatherless; uphold the cause of the poor and the oppressed."

Song: "Could Have Been" - Kirk Franklin, J Moss, and Tye Tribbett

A Prayer for Our Coworkers and Workplace

Heavenly Father,
Thank You for placing us in this workplace—not just to earn a living, but to be light, love, and purpose in action. Today, I lift up my coworkers to You. Bless them with peace in their hearts, clarity in their tasks, and joy in their contributions. May our workplace be more than just a building—it becomes a space of collaboration, growth, and grace.

Lord Jesus, You worked with Your hands, walked among people, and built relationships with compassion. Help us to follow Your example. When tensions rise, give us patience. When misunderstandings occur, give us humility. Let our words be seasoned with kindness and our actions reflect Your love. May we honor one another and build each other up.

Holy Spirit, fill our workplace with unity and wisdom. Guide our decisions, protect our integrity, and inspire creativity. Let our team be known for excellence, empathy, and encouragement. Help us to see each other not just as coworkers, but as fellow image-bearers of God. May our work be fruitful, our relationships be strong, and our atmosphere be filled with Your presence.

In Jesus Name,

AMEN

Action:

- Write a short message to a coworker thanking them for something they've done or simply for who they are.
- Take 60 seconds during your workday to pray silently for your team's peace and productivity.

Affirmation:

"I am a source of peace and encouragement in my workplace; I honor my coworkers and serve with grace."

Scriptures:

- Colossians 3:23–24 — "Whatever you do, work at it with all your heart, as working for the Lord…"
- Ephesians 4:2–3 — "Be completely humble and gentle… Make every effort to keep the unity of the Spirit…"
- Proverbs 27:17 — "As iron sharpens iron, so one person sharpens another."

Song: "Better" - Jessica Reedy

A Prayer to Heal the World

Heavenly Father,
You are the Creator of every nation, every soul, and every heartbeat. In a world fractured by war, injustice, disease, and division, we cry out for Your healing. Let Your mercy flow across borders and boundaries. Touch the broken places—both seen and unseen—and restore what hatred, greed, and fear have torn apart. We ask for Your peace to reign where chaos has taken root, and for Your love to mend what violence has shattered.

Lord Jesus, You walked among the hurting, the hungry, and the hopeless. You healed with compassion and led with truth. Teach us to do the same. Help us to be agents of healing in our communities, our countries, and our conversations. When despair feels louder than hope, remind us that You have overcome the world. Let Your light shine through us, illuminating paths of reconciliation, justice, and grace.

Holy Spirit, Breathe unity into our divisions. Stir up compassion where apathy has settled. Guide leaders with wisdom, protect the vulnerable with power, and awaken hearts to Your presence. Heal the earth from sickness, the people from hatred, and the systems from corruption. May revival rise from the ashes, and may Your Spirit move across the globe with healing in its wings.

In Jesus Name,

AMEN

<u>Action:</u>

- Choose one country or crisis to pray for each day. Speak healing, peace, and restoration over it.
- Reach out to someone from a different background or belief system. Listen, learn, and love.

<u>Affirmation:</u>

"I am a vessel of healing and hope; through God's power, I help restore what is broken in the world."

<u>Scriptures:</u>

- 2 Chronicles 7:14 — "If my people… will humble themselves and pray… I will hear from heaven… and heal their land."
- John 14:27 — "Peace I leave with you; my peace I give you… Do not let your hearts be troubled."
- Isaiah 58:12 — "You will be called Repairer of Broken Walls, Restorer of Streets with Dwellings."

<u>Song:</u> "Hold On (Change is Comin') - Sounds of Blackness

<u>A Prayer for Hope</u>

Heavenly Father,
In moments when the light feels dim and the path uncertain, I turn to You—the God of hope, the anchor of my soul. Fill my heart with Your presence and remind me that even in the waiting, You are working. Let Your promises rise louder than my doubts, and Your peace settle deeper than my fears. Teach me to hope not in outcomes, but in You—the One who never fails.

Lord Jesus, You are the resurrection and the life, the proof that hope is never wasted. When I feel weary, remind me that You overcame. When I feel forgotten, remind me that You see me. Help me to hold on, even when the answers are delayed, and to trust that Your timing is perfect. Let my hope be rooted in Your love, not shaken by circumstances.

Holy Spirit, breathe fresh expectation into my spirit. Stir up joy where sorrow has lingered, and faith where fear has crept in. Help me to hope boldly, pray persistently, and believe fiercely. Let my life be a testimony of hope—hope that endures, hope that heals, hope that points others to You.

In Jesus Name,

AMEN

Action:

- Begin each day by saying, "My hope is in God, and He is faithful."
- Reflect on Romans 15:13 and Hebrews 6:19 throughout the week.
- Write a note of encouragement to someone who may need a reminder that hope is alive.

Affirmation:

"I am anchored in hope, sustained by grace, and expectant for all God has promised."

Scriptures:

- Romans 15:13 — "May the God of hope fill you with all joy and peace… so that you may overflow with hope."
- Hebrews 6:19 — "We have this hope as an anchor for the soul, firm and secure."
- Isaiah 40:31 — "Those who hope in the Lord will renew their strength…"
- Psalm 71:14 — "But as for me, I will hope continually and will praise You yet more and more."

Song: "I am Blessed" - Reed's Temple Choir

A Prayer for Finishing the Year Strong

Heavenly Father,
As this year draws to a close, I thank You for every moment—joyful and painful, clear and confusing. You've walked with me through it all, and now I ask for Your strength to finish well. Let me not coast or collapse, but rise with renewed focus and faith. Help me to tie up loose ends, honor my commitments, and reflect Your glory in every final step.

Lord Jesus, You completed Your mission with grace, endurance, and love. Teach me to do the same. When I feel weary, remind me that You are my strength. When I feel discouraged, remind me that You are my hope. Let me finish this year not just with accomplishments, but with alignment—with Your will, Your heart, and Your purpose.

Holy Spirit, breathe fresh energy into my spirit. Reveal what still needs my attention and what I can release. Help me to celebrate progress, forgive myself for missteps, and walk boldly into the new season. May I finish this year with gratitude, clarity, and peace—ready for what You're preparing next.

In Jesus Name,

AMEN

Action:

- Set aside time to journal what you've learned, overcome, and accomplished this year.
- Choose one unfinished task or goal and commit to completing it with prayer and intention.
- Each day until year-end, name one thing you're thankful for and one way God showed up.

Affirmation:

"I finish this year strong—with grace, purpose, and gratitude. God is with me in every step."

Scriptures:

- 2 Timothy 4:7 — "I have fought the good fight, I have finished the race, I have kept the faith."
- Philippians 3:14 — "I press on toward the goal to win the prize for which God has called me…"
- Hebrews 12:1–2 — "Let us run with perseverance the race marked out for us…"
- James 1:12 — "Blessed is the one who perseveres under trial…"

Song: "Trust in God - Elevation Worship (feat. Chris Brown)

A Prayer for Surrendering to What's Next

Heavenly Father,
You are the God who sees beyond what I can imagine. In this moment, I release the need to know every detail, every outcome, every step ahead. I surrender the weight of uncertainty and choose to rest in Your presence. Teach me to trust the silence, the stillness, the in-between. Let me find peace not in clarity, but in Your character—faithful, loving, and true.

Jesus,
You walked through unknown valleys with unwavering trust. You surrendered to the Father's will, even when the path led through pain. Help me do the same. When I feel restless, remind me that rest is not weakness—it's worship. When I feel anxious, whisper truth: that I am held, guided, and never alone. Let me lay down my striving and receive Your peace.

Holy Spirit, Be my anchor in the fog. Quiet the noise of doubt and distraction. Help me release control and embrace surrender—not as defeat, but as divine alignment. Show me how to prepare my heart for what's next, even if I don't yet know what it is. May I walk forward with open hands, soft heart, and steady faith.

In Jesus Name,

AMEN

Action:

- Set aside 10 minutes each day to sit in silence and breathe deeply. Whisper, "I trust You, Lord."
- Reflect on Isaiah 30:15 — "In quietness and trust is your strength."
- Write down what you're afraid to release. Then write, "I surrender this to God," and pray over each one.

Affirmation:

"I rest in God's presence and surrender the unknown; peace is my posture and trust is my strength."

Scriptures:

- Isaiah 30:15 — "In repentance and rest is your salvation, in quietness and trust is your strength…"
- Proverbs 3:5–6 — "Trust in the Lord with all your heart… and He will make your paths straight."
- Psalm 46:10 — "Be still, and know that I am God."
- Romans 8:28 — "In all things God works for the good of those who love Him…"

Song: "Moving Forward" - Ricardo Sanchez

A Prayer for Leaving a Legacy

Heavenly Father,
You are the God of generations—the One who sees beyond my lifetime and into eternity. Today, I ask You to help me live a life that leaves a legacy of faith, love, and purpose. Let my words, actions, and decisions echo Your truth long after I'm gone. May the seeds I plant today bloom in the hearts of those who come after me.

Lord Jesus, You left a legacy of grace, sacrifice, and redemption. Teach me to live with that same intentionality. Help me to pour into others, to mentor with compassion, and to serve with humility. Let my legacy not be built on titles or possessions, but on the lives I've touched and the truth I've lived. May my story point others to You.

Holy Spirit, guide me in shaping a legacy that honors Your presence. Help me to break generational curses and build generational blessings. Show me how to pass down wisdom, courage, and spiritual strength. Let my life be a bridge—connecting past faithfulness to future hope. May I leave behind not just memories, but momentum for the Kingdom.

In Jesus Name,

AMEN

Action:

- Write a letter to your future descendants sharing your faith, values, and hopes for them.
- Invest in someone younger—through mentorship, encouragement, or prayer.
- Reflect on Psalm 78:4 and 2 Timothy 2:2 to inspire generational impact.

Affirmation:

"I am building a legacy of faith, love, and purpose; my life will echo God's truth for generations to come."

Scriptures:

- Proverbs 13:22 — "A good person leaves an inheritance for their children's children…"
- Psalm 78:4 — "We will tell the next generation about the glorious deeds of the Lord…"
- 2 Timothy 2:2 — "Teach these truths to other trustworthy people who will be able to pass them on…"
- Deuteronomy 6:6–7 — "Repeat them again and again to your children…"

Song: "Better Than Good To Me" - Lady Harmony

A Prayer for Building and Loving a Chosen Family

Heavenly Father,
Thank You for the gift of chosen family—the souls You've woven into my life not by blood, but by divine connection. Teach me to love them deeply, intentionally, and without condition. Let my heart be a safe haven, my words a balm, and my presence a reminder that they are seen, valued, and cherished. May our bond reflect Your love—unbreakable, healing, and sacred.

Lord Jesus, You surrounded Yourself with friends, disciples, and seekers—people who became family through shared purpose and love. Help me to hold space for others the way You did: with compassion, patience, and grace. When someone needs to be heard, let me listen without judgment. When someone needs to be held, let me offer warmth without agenda. May I be a steady presence in the lives of those around me, honoring their journey and trusting Yours.

Holy Spirit, Lead me into deeper community—not just connection, but communion. Show me how to lean in when it's easier to pull away. Help me to build bridges, not walls; to nurture belonging, not performance. Let our lives consist of shared meals, honest conversations, and mutual growth. May I be a vessel of unity, a spark of joy, and a thread in the tapestry of collective healing.

In Jesus Name,

AMEN

Action:

- Reach out to someone in your chosen family today. Ask how they're really doing—and hold space for their truth.

Affirmation:

"I love with intention, hold space with grace, and lean into community with courage and joy."

Scriptures:

- Galatians 6:2 — "Carry each other's burdens, and in this way you will fulfill the law of Christ."
- Acts 2:44–46 — "All the believers were together and had everything in common… They broke bread in their homes and ate together with glad and sincere hearts."

Song: "The Question Is" - The Winans

Last Words

Thank you for being here.
I really hoped you enjoyed this book.
I pray that we are all blessed by it
and continue to grow in God.
Please share this book with someone you love.

Use the next pages to complete some of the actions,
create your own affirmations,
or even write your own prayers.

All of the songs selected and some of my personal
favorites, can be found on this playlist:

I will continue to pray for us all.

Love you Always,

Shirleena Racine

www.ingramcontent.com/pod-product-compliance
Lightning Source LLC
LaVergne TN
LVHW091127061026
849616LV00030B/290

* 9 7 9 8 9 9 3 0 7 6 3 0 0 *